Jesus as founder of a Platonic Christianity

The Message of the Gospel of Thomas

The author

Prof. Dr. Enno Edzard Popkes researches and teaches on the history and archeology of early Christianity and its environment at the faculty of Theology at the Kiel University. He is co-founder and chairman of the 'Kiel Academy of Thanatology e.V.' (www.kiath.de).

The concerns of the series 'Platonic Christianity'

Since its beginnings Christian theology has been shaped by influences of Platonism, which inspired various forms of 'Platonic Christianity'. The contributions of the series 'Platonic Christianity' take up these developments and present a new impulse for discussion: Those patterns of experience that are entitled with the (imprecise) term 'near-death experiences' nowadays have already shaped the emergence of Platonism and early Christianity. Scientific investigations regarding the phenomenon 'death' in general and regarding so-called 'near-death experiences' in particular open up approaches to new forms of a Platonic-Christian religiosity.

Platonic Christianity 2

Jesus as founder of a Platonic Christianity

The Message of the Gospel of Thomas

Enno Edzard Popkes

Bibliographic information of the German National Library:
The Deutsche Nationalbibliothek lists this publication in the
Deutsche Nationalbibliografie; detailed bibliographic data can be
found on the Internet at http://dnb.dnb.de .

Typesetting and layout: Gerhild Schiller

© 2020 Popkes, Enno Edzard
Herstellung und Verlag: BoD – Books on Demand, Norderstedt
ISBN: 9783751972024

Contents

Preface

The edition of volumes of the series 'Platonic Christianity' is dedicated to the following concerns: On the one hand, I would like to outline in a generally understandable language essential results of my studies regarding the history of early Christianity, Platonism, and so-called 'near-death experiences'. On the other hand, I want to stimulate a discussion that can only be conducted in an interdisciplinary and transdisciplinary manner[1]. Both concerns are connected by a basic idea, which can be summarized as follows: Since its beginnings, Christian theology has been shaped by influences of Platonism, which inspired various forms of 'Platonic Christianity'. The contributions of the series 'Platonic Christianity' takes up these developments and present a new impulse for discussion: Those patterns of experiences that are entitled with the (imprecise) term 'near-death experiences' nowadays have already shaped the development of Platonism and early Christianity. Scientific investigations regarding the phenomenon 'death' in general and regarding so-called 'near-death experiences' in particular open up approaches to new forms of Platonic-Christian religiosity. The main features of this approach are set out in the first five volumes. First, the historical background, methodology and terminology will be presented on which all the following subvolumes are based on: (*Volume 1: Platonic Christianity: Historical and Methodological Foundations*). The second volume shows how early the first forms of Platonic Christianity can be observed. This is explained by the interpretation of the figure and message of Jesus as handed down by the Gospel of Thomas (*Volume 2: Jesus as Founder of a Platonic Christianity: the Message of the Gospel of Thomas*). Essential backgrounds of this concept are presented in

---

1   In order to facilitate interdisciplinary and transdisciplinary connectivity, subject-specific discourses are only documented to a limited extent. With regard to detailed subject-specific discourses, I refer to my preliminary work and research projects that are listed in the bibliography or footnotes.

the third volume with a sketch of Plato's theology (*Volume 3: The Theology of Plato: Backgrounds of a Platonic Christianity*). Against this background, it will be explained to what extent the Gospel of Thomas and the Gospel of John form contrasting parallels that reveal the potentials and conflicts which can be inspired by a Platonic Christianity (*Volume 4: The Gospel of Thomas and the Gospel of John: Revivals of an Early Christian Discourse*). The fifth volume opens up the new perspective on this topic, which will be developed in the following volumes (*Volume 5: Near Death Experiences: Platonic-Christian Interpretations*).

Guiding assumption of the contributions of the series 'Platonic Christianity': Scientific investigations regarding the phenomenon of 'death' in general and regarding so-called 'near-death experiences' in particular open up approaches to new forms of Platonic-Christian religiosity.

Many people participated in the completion of these volumes. This applies not only to my assistants, who were involved in the difficulties of proofreading. It also applies to many friends and family members, whom I have repeatedly confronted with the question of whether I could 'translate' the scientific language familiar to me into a generally comprehensible language. I would like to thank in particular Sarah Perez Kuwald, Swantje Rinker, Jasmin Reschka-Zielke, Femke Schiller, Gerhild Schiller, Ullrich Schiller, Dr. Stephanie Gripentrog-Schedel, Tim Schedel, Alexander Gripentrog, Andreas Gripentrog and – last, but not least – my mother Maria Luise Popkes-Wilts.

Kiel-Kronshagen, Spring 2020   Enno Edzard Popkes

1. Purpose and structure

Jesus had disciples. Without a doubt, one disciple was called Thomas. However, the relationship between Jesus and Thomas is a debatable point. The 'Gospel of Thomas' claims to convey secret sayings of Jesus which the teacher entrusted to that disciple. They often differ noticeably from Jesus' sayings which are handed down in the New Testament. This raises fundamental questions: What is the message of the Gospel of Thomas? What significance does it have for understanding the words and deeds of Jesus? What significance does the Gospel of Thomas have for the understanding of early Christianity? Why does the Gospel associated with the name of John present Thomas as a doubter who is skeptical of Jesus and does not believe in his bodily resurrection?

These first questions already give an idea why the Gospel of Thomas can ignite massive disputes, which are observed far beyond the borders of theology and church. Above all, however, these questions due to a further question that can be formulated in different variations. On the one hand, it can be put hypothetically in relation to the past: *What would have happened if those interpretations of Jesus' message handed down in the Gospel of Thomas had shaped the development of Christianity in the same way as the biblical writings?* On the other hand, it can be formulated as a question that has concrete consequences for the present and the future: *What does it mean when this interpretation of Jesus' message is reconsidered?*

The present book puts one answer to this last question up for discussion: *The Gospel of Thomas offers a Platonic interpretation of the figure and message of Jesus that can inspire new forms of Platonic-Christian religiosity.*

> _Guiding assumption 2.1:_ The Gospel of Thomas is one of the oldest witnesses of a Platonic Christianity. Its message should be reconsidered today.

This assumption will be explained as follows: First, basic information is conveyed which is important for the understanding of the Gospel of Thomas (chapter 2). Then it is explained in what way the figure and the message of Jesus is interpreted in a platonic manner in the Gospel of Thomas, namely regarding five topics which appear regularly in the sayings of Jesus. The titles of the chapters first allude to a partial aspect of a saying (in the sense of the chosen order it is Gos. Thom. 3:4; 108:1; 77:1; 24:3; 50:1). Those partial aspects already show central statements of the Gospel of Thomas:

"If you recognize yourselves ..."

"... you will become like me."

"I am the light ..."

"... and it enlightens the whole world."

"We have come out of the light ..."

The subtitles of the chapters emphasize basics ideas of those sayings. These are 'revelation by self-knowledge' (chapter 3), 'oneness with Jesus' (chapter 4), 'the origin and perfection of creation' (chapter 5), 'enlightenment of the world' (chapter 6) and 'transmigration of souls' (chapter 7). Finally, the central features of the Platonic interpretation of the figure and the message of Jesus are summarized again and illustrated schematically (chapter 8).

2. Introduction

Before an interpretation of the Gospel of Thomas is put up for discussion, basic information about the historical background and the structure of this work must be given. First of all, it is necessary to think about a fact, which is of central importance for scientific considerations of the history of early Christianity. The Bible is – as its Greek name *ta biblia* ('the books') already suggests – actually a library. It bears testimonies written by people who lived in different times, regions and historical contexts. This also applies to the second part of the Bible, which commonly is entitled with the 'New Testament'. It is a collection of writings that provide important insights into the history of early Christianity. But the history of Christianity was much more complex than the New Testament suggests. This applies particulary to the disciple of Jesus who will be examined in more detail below; that is to say Thomas and the Gospel associated with his name. For this reason, the contrast between biblical and non-biblical traditions about Thomas is first of all explained. On the one hand it is outlined in what way Thomas was stylized in the Gospel of John as the symbol of a doubter who was sceptical about Jesus' message and who did not want to believe in the bodily resurrection of Jesus (2.1). On the other hand, extra-biblical traditions about Thomas and the so-called 'Thomas Christianity' are being explained (2.2). It must also be clarified why the Gospel of Thomas was suppressed in antiquity and how it was rediscovered in the 20th century (2.3). It is then shown why not only the individual sayings of Jesus in the Gospel of Thomas are mysterious, but why the work itself remains mysterious (2.4). Against this background the differences between the image of Jesus in the Gospel of Thomas and the biblical Gospels are explained (2.5), especially the images of Jesus in the Gospel of Thomas and the Gospel of John (2.6). Likewise, the basic problems of a religio-historical classification of the Gospel of Thomas and of its references to platonic traditions must be adressed (2.7 and 2.8). The latter leads to a question which, in my opinion, has been overlooked in previous discourses: What significance do the contrasts between the Gospel of Thomas and the Gospel of John have for the question of the so-called 'Historical Jesus'? (2.9). At the end of the introduction, the translation and structure of the text witnesses of the Gospel of Thomas are explained (2.10).

2.1 Thomas, the doubter?

What significance did Thomas have for the development of early Christianity? This question can be answered in different ways. If one looks only at the collection of writings called the 'New Testament', one can come to the conclusion that Thomas was almost meaningless. Such an assessment, however, changes fundamentally when those testimonies are considered, which have not been included in the New Testament. In extra-biblical traditions, Thomas is portrayed as a special disciple of Jesus, to whom various Christian communities refer.

The opposing pictures of Thomas can be traced as follows: All the gospels included in the canon of the New Testament emphasize that there was a person named Thomas among the disciples of Jesus (cf. Mark 3:16-19//Matt 10:2-4//Luke 6:13-16). They also agree in that he belonged to a special group, namely the circle of twelve disciples that Jesus is said to have called the apostles. In the Gospels, which have been associated with the names Matthew, Mark and Luke, Thomas otherwise receives no further attention. This also corresponds to the narratives of the Acts of the Apostles as an immediate continuation of the Gospel of Luke (Act 1:13).

Only one single scripture in the New Testament mentions Thomas more than once – but this reference is all the more important. In the Gospel of John a picture of Thomas presented, making him the symbol of a doubter. He was sceptical about the message of his teacher and did not understand it properly (John 11:16; 14:4-5; 20:24-29). This especially refers to the belief in a bodily resurrection of Jesus. But the image of the doubting Thomas also forms the background against which the author of the Gospel of John stages the climax of his work. Thomas is said to have demanded to see the resurrected Jesus with his own eyes and to touch the wounds of his crucifixion. Otherwise, he could not believe in his physical resurrection. According to the Fourth Gospel, this demand was met. As a result, the 'Johannine Thomas' formulates the highest creed handed down in the New Testament writings. The former doubter Thomas finally addresses Jesus as 'his Lord and his God' (John 20:28)[2].

The dramaturgy of this narrative implies one question: Was there a special reason why the author of the Gospel of John depicted the figure of Thomas as the symbol of a doubter? This question also comes to mind when we consider the other Gospels in the New Testament in which Thomas is not made stand out in this way. However, it gains importance when extra-biblical writings and traditions are included in the discussion. By doing so the impression arises that the author of the Gospel of John wanted to criticize and correct an important authority of early Christianity and its interpretation of the figure and message of Jesus[3]. Even if the surviving text witnesses of the Gospel of Thomas are relative-

---

2   As many other commentators H. Thyen, Johannesevangelium, 767 marks John 20:28-29 as the most important confession and the climax of the fourth gospel: "Dies ist das adäquateste und gefüllteste Bekenntnis des gesamten Evangeliums. In ihm gipfeln alle bisherigen Prädikationen Jesu, und zugleich werden hier die Aussagen des Prologs ... wieder eingeholt".

3   For similar assessments cf. J. G. Riley, Resurrection, passim; A. D. DeConick, Voices, passim; S. Witischeck, Thomas, 211ff.; 256ff.; 356ff.; J. Hartenstein, Charakterisierung, 262; E. Pagels, Geheimnis, passim; I. Dunderberg, Disciple, passim; S. J. Patterson, Way, 148-152.

ly young[4], the literary stylization of the figure of Thomas in the Gospel of John is an indication that a specific teaching tradition was associated with this disciple of Jesus.

Guiding assumption 2.2: The author of the Gospel of John stylizes Thomas as the symbol of a doubter in order to criticize a contrary interpretation of the figure and message of Jesus.

2.2 Thomas and Thomas-Christianity

Christian communities, often referred to as 'Thomas-Christianity', still exist today. This term is of course misleading, as it is not an official self-designation. The so-called 'Thomas Christianity' is not a uniform denomination with independent confessions and institutions. It is rather a collective term for different groups, which claim to go back to the missionary activities of this special disciple of Jesus[5].

Guiding assumption 2.3: The collective term 'Thomas-Christianity' describes different religious communities which refer to the Apostle Thomas and which are not represented by the writings of the New Testament.

---

4   Regarding attempts of a reconstruction of earlier versions of the Gospel of Thomas cf. A. D. DeConick, The Original Gospel, passim. For similar assessments cf. J. G. Riley, Resurrection, passim; A. D. DeConick, Voices, passim; S. Witischeck, Thomas, 211ff.; 256ff. bzw. 356ff.; J. Hartenstein, Charakterisierung, 262; E. Pagels, Geheimnis, passim; I. Dunderberg, Disciple, passim; S. J. Patterson, Way, 148-152. For critical denials of those attempts cf. among others W. Eisele, Thomas, passim; J. Schröter, Thomas, 492ff.

5   Concering the complex and sometimes heterogeneous history of such communities and traditions cf. J. Thomaskutty, Saint Thomas, passim; J. Tubach, Elemente, passim; S. Gathercole, Thomas, 144ff; H.-P. Poirier, Thomas, 295ff; P. Sellew, Thomas Christianity, 11ff; B. Layton, Gnostic Scriptures, 362f; H. J. W. Drijvers, Thomasakten, 291; G. Garitte, Thomas, 497ff; R. Uro, Thomas, 10ff etc.

Many of those communities claim that Thomas carried his teacher's message all the way to India. He arrived in the south of India at the middle of the first century and died there as a martyr at the beginning of the 70s. Even today there are various places of worship in South India that commemorate the mission and death of Thomas. However, from a historica point of view it is hardly possible to distinguish between reliable historical information and legendary narratives in these diverse traditions. Nevertheless, it is difficult to deny one aspect: There was a disciple of Jesus called Thomas who spread the message of his teacher to regions that receive little or no attention in New Testament writings.

The complexity of different traditions about Thomas also corresponds to the fact that different writings claim his authority. Of course, they differ clearly from each other, both formally and in terms of content. They give an idea of different ideas associated with the name Thomas. Thus, for example, the so-called 'Infancy Gospel of Thomas', which must not be confused with the gospel of Thomas, reports supposed events in the life of the young Jesus. They are intended to illustrate the divine power and extraordinary knowledge that Jesus is said to have had already as a child. Many of these legends may seem peculiar to today's readers (e.g. the well-known story that little Jesus played at a stream, made birds out of clay and brought them to life). However, they correspond to many ancient legends, which have later embellished the narratives of important personalities' childhoods. The fact that things were no different with Jesus is already documented in the biblical gospels (this applies above all to the legends about the birth of Jesus) and many other stories that were widespread in antiquity. However, the 'Infancy Gospel of Thomas' does not answer a question that is of interest for an interpretation of the Gospel of Thomas: Why would Thomas be one of those persons who could pass on these events? The figure of Thomas is not examined in detail in the 'Childhood Gospel of Thomas'. The situation is different with other early Christian writings in which the figure of

Thomas is central to the narratives. Thus e.g. different variants of the so-called 'Acts of Thomas' were handed down, which probably originated only in the third century. They combine different narratives about Thomas, who wants to describe his actions and experiences on his way to India. Likewise in the Old Church there were various versions of a so-called 'Apocalypse of Thomas' that claim to announce imminent events, which would precede the expected end of the world.

What the scriptures mentioned so far have in common is that they hardly address the relationship between Jesus and Thomas as teacher and disciple. However, this is at the centre of two writings found alongside with the Nag Hammadi Codices. Before the background to this discovery can be explained in the following step, it is necessary to anticipate a phenomenon that contradicts the image of Thomas as a doubter drawn by author of the Gospel of John. In the context of the Nag Hammadi writings not only the Gospel of Thomas was rediscovered, but also the previously unknown 'Book of Thomas'. It is certainly no coincidence that this writing was also handed down in the second codex (NHC II,7). According to its literary design, the 'Book of Thomas' claims to give an account of a conversation that Jesus is said to have had with Thomas before his return to heaven. Thomas is addressed by Jesus as "my twin and my only true friend" (NHC II,7 138:9-10). He is thus declared the most important disciple of Jesus. Such a relationship between Jesus and Thomas is also assumed in the Gospel of Thomas, which can now be examined more closely.

2.3 The Suppression and Rediscovery of the Gospel of Thomas

In the preceding explanations, the peculiarity of the depiction of Thomas by the author of the Gospel of John was described. It raises the question of whether there were disputes about the figure of Thomas at the end of the first century. This impression gains considerable weight when the following is taken into consideration: Since the time of early Christianity it has been known that there was a 'Gospel of Thomas'. It has been mentioned, quoted and criticized by various authors (including Hippolytus, Origen, Eusebius, etc.[6]). Nevertheless, the Gospel of Thomas was lost for a long time. This did not change until 1945, when Egyptian fellahs accidentally found a jar about one metre in size, which was carefully hidden in impassable terrain[7]. In this vessel there were at least thirteen codices (this is the name of a form of books already developed in antiquity). Since the site was not far from the Upper Egyptian town of Nag-Hammadi, these writings have since been referred to as the Nag-Hammadi scriptures or the Nag-Hammadi codices.

The external circumstances of the find suggest that those writings were not 'waste paper' to be disposed of. It is much more likely that they should be saved from destruction in a save place. The individual codices were wrapped into leather envelopes and additionally surrounded by other protective materials. A letter correspondence that seems to offer an insight into the social backgrounds from which the Nag Hammadi writings originated was among them. This could be a monastery situated near Šeneset (Chenoboskion). Since this monastery is only about ten kilometres away from the place where those writings were found, it can be assumed that the Nag Hammadi writings originate from such

---

6   For corresponding quotations and allusions see S. C. Carlson, Use, 137-151; S. Gathercole, Thomas, 35ff. and 62-90; H. W. Attridge, Greek Fragments, 103ff.; D. Lührmann, Fragmente, 106-108.

7   The circumstances of the discovery cannot be clearly reconstructed. There is evidence that other codices have not been properly handled or even destroyed by their finders. J. M. Robinson, Coptic Manuscript, passim; idem, Discovery, 206ff.; B. A. Pearson, Nag Hammadi, 982ff.

a monastery. They may have been copied and studied by monks[8]. However, the location of the discovery and the chronological indications are revealing. Both the dates of that correspondence and the analyses of the materials of the codices indicate that these texts were copied or translated in the first half of the fourth century. This is remarkable because this period is pertinent to the history of the development of the New Testament canon. In the year 367 CE Athanasius, the bishop of Alexandria, wrote his 39th Easter Letter. In this letter, Athanasius determined which written testimonies of early Christianity were and were not a legitimate basis for worship and theological reflection. This selection can already be partly seen in earlier forms of canon formation and it was gradually adopted in other regions and ministries of the Old Church. Thus, way a large number of testimonies of early Christianity were declared illegitimate. For this reason, the instructions formulated by Athanasius in his 39th Easter Letter may have given grounds for hiding the Nag Hammadi writings and could explain why the Gospel of Thomas was lost for so long[9].

The Nag Hammadi writings thus made a complete version of the Gospel of Thomas accessible again. It has been integrated as the

---

8   Regarding the backgrounds within the history of monasticism cf. H. Lundhaug/J. Lance, Monastic Origins, passim; C. Markschies, Nag-Hammadi writings, 15-36. On earlier stages of discourses see J. W. B. Barns/G. M. Brown/J. C. Shelton, Cartonnage, 142-144. cf. H. Bacht, Vermächtnis II, 20; 25f.; F. Wisse, Early Monasticism, 431ff.

9   Vgl. C. W. Hedrick, Gnostic Proclivities, 94: "Prior to Athanasius' proclamations they were probably regarded by the visionaries like the 'other books', not included in the canon but yet approved by the fathers to be read for ‚instruction in the word of the godlines', i. e., the Wisdom of Salomon, the Wisdom of Sirach, Esther, Judith, Tobit, the Teaching of the Apostles and the Shepard. Although the collection of books used by the visionaries would probably not have been approved reading for a monk, it was at least not officially forbidden reading until after A. D. 367. After this date the books could no longer be used in the monasteries … because the Bishop has prohibited it." Regarding the backgrounds of term like 'canonical', 'non-canonical' or 'apocryphal' cf. C. Tuckett, Name, 149-164; T. Nicklas, Christian Apokrypha, 23-38; H.-J. Klauck, Umwelt II, 155; H. Lundhaug/J. Lance, Monastic Origins, 146f. bzw. 172-174; C. Markschies, Nag-Hammadi-Schriften, 18f.

second script in the second Codex (for this reason this text version is referred to as NHC II,2). Nevertheless, this copy is a Coptic translation, i.e. a version of the work in the language of the Egyptian Christians. However and without a doubt, this was not the language in which the Gospel of Thomas was originally written. This is supported not only by linguistic evidence, but also by further fragments of the work. They were found at the turn of the 19th to the 20th century, within the context of the so-called Oxyrhynchus-Papyri. Since the term 'Gospel of Thomas' was not present in these fragments, they could only be identified as older Greek variants of the Gospel of Thomas by comparison with the Coptic translation (these are designated with the abbreviations P.Oxy 1:1-42/654:1-42/655 [d] 1-5). Since there are sometimes clear differences between the individual text witnesses, strictly speaking one cannot actually speak of *the* Gospel of Thomas, but only of 'traditions of the Gospel of Thomas'[10].

Even though all the surviving text witnesses of the Gospel of Thomas were found in Egypt, there are various indications that its spiritual roots also lie in Syrian Christianity. These are, among other things, linguistic indications, similarities with those Thomas traditions mentioned in the preceding step, and other testimonies of Syrian Christianity (cf. the so-called 'Diatessaron', i.e. the attempt to harmonize the four New Testament Gospels, which was written by the Syrian theologian Tatian around 170 AD)[11]. However, the discussion becomes even more complex against the back-

---

10   Since there are clear differences between the individual textual witnesses, we cannot actually speak of the Gospel of Thomas, but only of traditions of the Gospel of Thomas (cf. W. Eisele, Thomas, 250). This is a critical demarcation of attempts to reconstruct an original version of the Gospel of Thomas, for which there are no valid textual witnesses. Regarding such an attempt, see A. D. DeConick, The Original Gospel, passim.

11   For this discussion see e.g. N. Perrin, Tatian, passim; idem, Aramaic Origins, 50-59. If the basis of the discussion will not change because of further text findings, the assessment of S. Gathercole, Thomas, 110f. will hardly change: "In the end, then, it is probably best to admit our ignorance about Thomas's provenance, while acknowledging that Syria and Egypt are reasonable possibilities."

ground of the following question: To what extent are the ideas handed down by the Gospel of Thomas indirectly addressed in earlier Christian testimonies? While the literary stylization of the figure of Thomas in the Gospel of John reveals already advanced levels of reflection, several sayings of the Gospel of Thomas act as contrasting parallels to ideas that are already mentioned in the Pauline epistles (cf. Gos. Thom. 51/1 Cor 15:12 regarding the understanding of resurrection; Gos. Thom. 83-84/1 Cor 15:46-49 regarding the distinction of different aspects of the creation of human beings; Gos. Thom. 77/1 Cor 8:5-6 regarding the origin of creation; Gos. Thom. 2:4/1 Cor 4:8 regarding the motif of reign and the affinities between Gos. Thom. 17 and 1 Cor 2:9).

> _Guiding assumption 2.4:_ Even if its surviving text witnesses and traditions are relatively young and show gradual growth, the Gospel of Thomas represents positions within early Christian discourses that occur indirectly already in canonical testimonies.

From the point of view of the history of religion, the Gospel of Thomas is of highest value, as are many other testimonies of the Nag Hammadi writings. These writings offer access to alternative forms of early Christianity, which were suppressed in the process of the formation of the New Testament canon and dogmatic teachings[12]. Their peculiarities can only be adequately understood if they are not measured against those Christian concepts

---

12   Cf. A. D. DeConick, The Original Gospel, 5f., who understands the Gospel of Thomas as a testimony of early Christian mysticism: "An ancient 'Orthodox' Syrian Gospel: this is the historical context for the Christianity described in the Gospel of Thomas. The sayings in this little book describe a mystical form of Christianity in which the believer worked not just to understand God, but to 'know' him in the deepest and intimate sense. They wished to _experience_ God immediately and directly. The Thomasine Christians teach us in their Gospel that the first step toward this Ultimate experience is to achive a personal state of passionlessnes. Complete control over their bodies garnered for them the condition necessary to storm the gates of Eden."

which have finally prevailed in the history of Christianity – or to put it more precisely: which have been prevailed. For this reason, various voices are now calling for the Gospel of Thomas to be understood as the 'fifth gospel' and to be appreciated in theological reflections and churchly contexts[13]. The Gospel of Thomas thus paradigmatically emphasizes the extent to which 'hidden discourses' can be observed between canonical and extra-canonical testimonies of early Christianity, whose revivals can, in my opinion, give theology and church valuable stimulus[14].

> _Guiding assumption 2.5:_ Apocryphal testimonies such as the Gospel of Thomas reveal early Christian discourses that should be revived today.

Even if the Gospel of Thomas is explicitly classified as a Gospel by the _subscriptio_ following the last saying Gos. Thom. 114, it differs clearly from the New Testament Gospels, both in its formal structure and in its message. These differences are explained in the following two chapters.

2.4 The Structure of the Gospel of Thomas

The Gospel of Thomas claims to convey 'secret sayings' of Jesus. But not only the individual sayings seem mysterious. The Gospel of Thomas itself is surrounded by many mysteries. This already applies to the question of who this Jesus should actually be. If

---

13 Regarding the term 'Fifth Gospel' cf. S. J. Patterson/J. M. Robinson (Ed.), Fifth Gospel, passim.

14 For the structure and concerns of this concept, see E. E. Popkes, Platonic Christianity, Chapter 3 or 4. Representative for many other assessments regarding the Gospel of Thomas G. Theissen, Religion, 284f. states: "When it was not accepted in the canon, a valuable variant of the primitive Christian faith was lost: an individual primitive Christian mysticism. (...) it embodies in a pure form the message of the infinitive value of the individual human soul. (...) It speaks to individuals and the solitary. And it offers them a mysticism of union with God, a return to where everything comes from."

one would not presuppose the stories of the biblical gospels when reading the Gospel of Thomas, then it would be completely unclear when and where Jesus acted.

The formal structure of the Gospel of Thomas also raises many questions. The prologue emphasizes that Thomas wrote down Jesus' secret sayings. This is followed by 114 separate texts. For the most part they are introduced with the formula 'Jesus says'. Questions by the disciples of Jesus are rarely mentioned. Dialogues are almost completely missing[15]. A thematic order of the sayings cannot be recognized either. Individual words of Jesus are connected by keywords and motifs. They can follow each other directly, but they can also be arranged separately. In contrast to the biblical gospels, which present the words and deeds of Jesus in the context of elaborated narratives, the Gospel of Thomas sometimes seems like a disordered box of notes. For this reason, it has often been related to the so-called 'Sayings Gospel' or 'Saying Source', which is denoted by the abreviation 'Q'[16].

Since the beginnings of historical-critical considerations of the biblical writings, the relationship between the Gospels has been discussed. Already in the middle of the 19th century, the main features of the so-called 'Two-Source-Hypothesis' were developed, which is still – in different variations – represented in the majority of research today. Its central thesis consists in the assumption that the authors of the Gospels of Matthew and Luke each knew (possibly different) versions of the Gospel of Mark. They also used written collections of the words of Jesus, which they incorporated in different ways into the narrative of the Gospel of Mark. The hypothesis of the existence of a written collection of the words of

---

15   This phenomenon had been interpreted convincingly by C. W. Hedrick, Thomas, 11: "Certain sayings seem to assume a user community (sayings 25, 26, 39a, 40, and 99), but generally Thomas reflects a universalism inviting anyone to share in its religious views by discovering the right interpretation of the words of Jesus (saying 1) ...".

16   For a sketch of the this discussion see S. Gathercole, Thomas, 29-32.

Jesus was thus formulated almost 100 years before the rediscovery of the Gospel of Thomas. Against this background, the formal structure of the Gospel of Thomas is all the more remarkable: the Gospel of Thomas is such a collection of Jesus' words. Because of this, the relationship between the Gospel of Thomas and the 'Sayings Gospel' or 'Saying Scource' is still a controversial issue even to the present day. And also these discussions lead again to the question how old the Gospel of Thomas is.

Even more peculiar is the formal structure of the Gospel of Thomas, if the following problem is taken into consideration: Many words of Jesus in the Gospel of Thomas are not really 'secret'. Rather, they have clear parallels in the biblical gospels. Thus, they do not seem to be 'secret' words of Jesus. Rather, they are mysterious because their meaning is not immediately apparent.

The aspects described raise many questions: Why does the Gospel of Thomas pay so little attention to the life and death of Jesus? Is this because, like Paul's letters, it is one of the oldest writings of early Christianity? Paul also hardly mentions the life and deeds of Jesus. He assumes that his readers know about it. Is this also the case with the Gospel of Thomas? And what is the relationship between the words of Jesus in the Gospel of Thomas and the Gospels of the Bible? Is the lack of structure and framing also an indication that it transmits very ancient forms of Jesus' words? Is the Gospel of Thomas completely independent of the Biblical Gospels or are there indications of mutual influences? Such questions have been controversially discussed since the discovery of this work. But why these controversies attract so much attention has to do with a further question that continuously accompanies the aforementioned remarks: Does the Gospel of Thomas convey an interpretation of the figure and message of Jesus, which rightly refers to Jesus himself? The eminent dimension of this question only becomes apparent when not only the formal differences between the Biblical Gospels and the Gospel of Thomas are considered, but also their differences in content.

2.5 Differences between the Images of Jesus in the Biblical Gospels and in the Gospel of Thomas

Who was the historical figure of Jesus of Nazareth? What was his message? Who has appropriately interpreted the message of Jesus? Such questions have been formulated in many variations since the time of early Christianity, and even more since the beginnings of historical-critical considerations of the biblical writings. However, they cannot be answered precisely. Rather, assumptions of research regarding the history of religion are only the expression of a *docta ignoratia*. In other words: From a scientific point of view, many aspects that are important for understanding the life and message of Jesus may never be clarified. But it can be explained why this is not possible[17]. In spite of this reservation a thesis can be formulated which is of importance for the understanding of the Gospel of Thomas: Even if the images of Jesus in the biblical Gospels are by no means uniform, they have central motives in common. These are fundamentally different from the interpretation of the figure and message of Jesus handed down by the Gospel of Thomas. But the differences between the Gospel of John and the Gospel of Thomas are particularly important.

> *Guiding assumption 2.6:* Even if the biblical gospels do not convey uniform images of Jesus, they are fundamentally different from the image of Jesus in the Gospel of Thomas.

The biblical gospels agree that Jesus did not only appear as an itinerant preacher. Rather, he claimed to be able to forgive people for their sins. He is said to have affirmed his message through

---

17 For insights into the history and topics of these complex as well as controversial questions cf. T. Holmén/S. E. Porter (Hg.), Jesus, passim; J. Schröter/C. Jacobi (ed.), Jesus Handbuch, passim; B. Chilton/C. A. Evans (Ed.), Jesus, passim; T. Holmén/S. E. Porter (Ed.), Jesus, passim; G. Theissen/A. Merz, Jesus, 21-30; S. J. Patterson, Historical Jesus, 233-249.

various healings and miracles. But forgiveness of sins, miracles and healings of Jesus are not mentioned in the Gospel of Thomas. Attention is paid exclusively to the sayings of Jesus.

The biblical gospels have in common the idea that hopes have been fulfilled in the words and deeds of Jesus as documented in the Jewish Bible. The Gospel of Thomas, on the other hand, makes no reference to the Jewish Bible. What this means can be explained using a striking example. The Jewish Bible documents hopes for a messianic figure whose arrival is to initiate a new reign of God. The biblical gospels have in common the idea that Jesus of Nazareth is this figure. Or to say it according to the Greek translation of these terms: Jesus is 'the Christ' who brings the kingdom of God. A central question in this matter is whether Jesus understood himself as such a Christ or whether he was only regarded as such by other persons. Also, in this respect the interpretation of the Gospel of Thomas differs fundamentally from the biblical images of Jesus: The title 'Christ' is mentioned neither directly nor indirectly in this work. The expectations associated with it do not correspond to the sayings of Jesus conveyed by the Gospel of Thomas.

Furthermore, the biblical images of Jesus agree that there were massive conflicts between Jesus and leading authorities of contemporary Judaism, culminating in his imprisonment in Jerusalem. Jesus was condemned by the Sanhedrin as a blasphemer and rebel and finally executed by command of the Roman prefect Pontius Pilate. On the other hand, the Gospel of Thomas does not pay any attention to the passion of Jesus.

The same applies to those narratives, which constitute the culmination and climax of the biblical gospels, namely the stories of a bodily resurrection of Jesus. These are completely missing in the Gospel of Thomas. An empty tomb of Jesus or encounters of the Risen One with his disciples are not mentioned. Nor would they correspond to the message of the Gospel of Thomas. Instead, traditional concepts of resurrection are even criticized.

Likewise, differences occur in regard to the understanding of the death of Jesus. The biblical gospels emphasize in different ways that the death of Jesus is an atoning sacrifice. God himself had redefined his relationship to his creation through the vicarious death of his son. For the most part, these interpretations are based on concepts regarding sacrifices and atonement, which are documented in the Jewish Bible. Even such ideas are again completely absent in the Gospel of Thomas.

> _Guiding assumption 2.7:_ For the Gospel of Thomas, the historical circumstances of the life of Jesus, the faith in Jesus as Christ, the interpretation of the death of Jesus as atonement and the faith in a bodily resurrection of Jesus have no relevance.

2.6 The Gospel of Thomas and the Gospel of John as antagonists

The differences outlined in the previous chapters can be spotted between the Gospel of Thomas and all biblical Gospels. The greatest differences, however, can be observed between the Gospel of John and the Gospel of Thomas[18]. In the Gospel of John, various ideas are significantly developed, which are noticable in older testimonies of early Christianity only rudimentarily. This is especially true for the deification of Jesus and for the interpretation of the death of Jesus as a death of atonement.

---

18 The relationship between the Gospel of John and the Gospel of Thomas has often been controversially discussed since the discovery of the Naq Hammadi Codices. On the history of research and on the sketch of various explanations, see, among others, S. Witischeck, Thomas, passim; S. Gathercole, Thomas, 64f.; 176ff.; E. E. Popkes, Licht, passim; G. J. Riley, Resurrection, passim; A. D. DeConick, Voices, passim; I. Dunderberg, Disciple, passim or S. J. Patterson, Way, 148-152, who aptly states: "But of all the New Testament writings, the closest to Thomas in both theology and worldview is the Gospel of John." (op. cit. 148).

More than in any other testimony of the biblical canon, Jesus is portrayed in John's Gospel as the incarnation of God. This is already emphasized by the prologue (John 1:1-3.14) and unfolded in the narration of the Fourth gospel. This shows impressively how far this image of Jesus is distanced from the historical figure of a Jewish itinerant preacher. The Jesus of the Gospel of John describes himself in a way that would be unimaginable and scandalous for Jewish people: He calls himself the Son of God who is 'one with his Father' (John 10:30). Whoever would see him would see that Father (John 14:9). The Johannine Jesus claims, that God had given him the power to give everlasting life (John 5:24-29). He could demonstrate his power by resurrecting corpses that were already decaying (John 11:38-44). The relationship of human beings to God would be determined by their relationship to him. Only those, who believe in Jesus as the Son of God will obtain eternal life and not be lost. Those who do not believe in him are already condemned (John 3:16-18). Here, too, the difference with the Gospel of Thomas becomes impressively apparent. There is no mention that the disciples have to believe in Jesus as the Son of God. The Jesus of the Gospel of Thomas rather demands his disciples to recognize themselves.

Within the Gospel of John, the figure of Jesus is depicted as being an incarnation of God that does not have an analogy in the synoptic gospels. An impressive example of this phenomenon is the interpretation of the death of Jesus. As the Son of God, Jesus has the power to give his life away and to take it back himself (John 10:17-18). He is the good shepherd who gives his life for his sheep (John 10:15). Jesus is the Lamb of God who carries the sin of the world (John 1:29). He is the bread of life given to the life of the world (John 6:51). Only those who eat his flesh and drink his blood will be given eternal life through him (John 6:53-56). Again, these features of the Gospel of John differ fundamentally from the interpretation of the message of Jesus handed down in the Gospel of Thomas. It does not understand the death of Jesus as a vicarious atonement death in the spirit of Jewish sacrificial rituals. But that eating the flesh and drinking the blood of Jesus should be a prerequisite for participation in eternal life would be grotesque and absurd in the sense of the Gospel of Thomas.

The sketched features of the Gospel of John draw a picture of Jesus that is without doubt already far removed from the historical figure of the Jewish itinerant preacher from Nazareth. This aspect may in turn give rise to a question: What prompted the author of the Fourth gospel to create such an image of Jesus? A historical critical view of the history of early Christianity offers different answers to this question. But there is one insight that unites them: Since the beginnings of early Christianity, different interpretations of the words and deeds of Jesus competed with each other. This can already be guessed from the individual testimonies of the collection of writings finally referred to as the 'New Testament'. However, these developments can only be adequately understood if extra-biblical scriptures are also considered. This applies especially to the Gospel of Thomas. The sketched features of the Gospel of John act as direct opposites to those interpretations of the figure and message of Jesus handed down by the Gospel of Thomas.

> _Guiding assumption 2.8:_ The image of Jesus in the Gospel of John can be interpreted as a direct contrast to the image of Jesus in the Gospel of Thomas.

For this reason, a guiding assumption can already made in advance, which will be established in the following explanations in various contexts: The Gospel of John can be understood as an alternative concept to the Gospel of Thomas. On the one hand, it depicts Thomas as a disciple of Jesus, who at first is said not to have understood his teacher. On the other hand, it illustrates another disciple of Jesus as the model of a supposed orthodoxy, who is not mentioned in the other biblical Gospels, namely the so-called 'Beloved Disciple' (John 13:23; 19:26f.; 20:2-10; 21:7)[19]. This figure is even referred to as the author of the Gospel (John 21:21-25)[20].

Behind these literary productions hides a controversy that has shaped the development of early Christianity. Sometimes the parallels or contrasting parallels are so striking that one can get the impression that authors, who had direct and vivid connections with each other, have gradually created these works[21].

Even if it is disputed to what extent these are literary fictions (for details see 2.9: The Gospel of Thomas, the Gospel of John and the 'Historical Jesus': a minor hint to a major problem), one aspect can be stated: Thomas represents an early Christian movement that is illegitimate from the point of view of the author of the Gospel of John. In terms of historical critism, the Gospel of Thomas testifies to a religiosity, which does not interpret the

---

19   The question of an identification of this figure was already discussed in early Christianity and it attracts the attention of exegetical discourses up to the present day. For a sketch of the history of research and contrary approaches to interpretation, see R. Bauckham, Disciple, 73-92; I. Dunderberg, Disciple, 116-148; J. Charlesworth, Disciple, passim; M. Hengel, Frage, 210-218 etc.

20   The understanding of John 21:24f. is of central importance for a historical-critical and discourse-analytical understanding of the Fourth Gospel. John 21:20-25 contains the thesis that the so-called 'Beloved Disciple' was the author of the Gospel of John. However, his work had to be edited by other people, since he had already died. These unidentified persons in turn testify to the credibility of the 'Beloved disciple' who is said to have been an eyewitness of Jesus (cf. John 21:24). This is the structure of the legitimation of the Gospel of John, if John 21:1-25 is interpreted as a supplement that was added to the original Gospel of John after the death of the 'Beloved disciple'. But if John 21:20-25 is interpreted as an original part of the Gospel of John, a different picture emerges: in this case, the testimony of credibility as an eyewitness would be part of the self-staging of the supposed author. Regarding the special importance of John 21 see among others H. Thyen, Johannesevangelium, 769ff.

21   Cf. S. Witetscheck, Johannes, 511: "Wir wissen nicht, ob sie sich persönlich kannten, aber die engen Kontakte ihrer Texte auf verschiedenen Ebenen bzw. Entwicklungsstufen sprechen dafür, dass die beiden Texte – das Johannesevangelium als redigierte Erzählung, das Thomasevangelium als Sammlung – in einem Zusammenhang entstanden sind, der nicht nur intellektueller, literar- und traditionsgeschichtlicher, sondern auch realer und sozialer Natur war."

words and deeds of Jesus against the background of the Jewish Bible. Rather, it is probably the oldest testimony of a 'Platonic Christianity' – and it represents Jesus as the founder of this movement.

> *Guiding assumption 2.9:* In the Gospel of Thomas, the figure and message of Jesus is interpreted not within the framework of biblical traditions, but within the framework of Platonism.

2.7 'Jesus meets Plato on the way to Gnosticism': the Gospel of Thomas within the history of early Christianity

Since the Gospel of Thomas was rediscovered, one question has been controversially discussed: How can such an interpretation of the figure and message of Jesus be located in the history of religion? The central problem can be illustrated with a metaphor: 'Jesus meets Plato on the way to Gnosticsm'. In this metaphor, two assessments, which have been formulated in different variations in previous interpretations of the Gospel of Thomas are related to each other[22]. It also illustrates the complexity of the encounters between Platonism and early Christianity. The meaning of the metaphor can be explained as follows: It is undisputed that the

---

22   The first aspect of the metaphor is formulated in a contribution to the discussion by S. J. Patterson, Plato, 205 with the programmatic title "Jesus meets Plato". Patterson comes to the following conclusion in relation to the Platonic motifs of the Gospel of Thomas: "What is clear, however, is that the *GThom* works with one of the dominant religious and philosophical schools of its days, Middle Platonism. In this sense, it stands near the beginning of what would become a long tradition of Platonic Christian theology, and is probably our earliest exemplar of such effort". The second aspect of the metaphor is coined by J. Schröter/H.-G. Bethge, Evangelium nach Thomas, 163, with the thesis that some sayings of the Gospel of Thomas reveal a "Jesusüberlieferung auf dem Weg zur Gnosis". For further surveys of platonic motifs within the Gospel of Thomas see also H. M. Jackson, Lion, passim; I. Miroshinkov, Plato, passim.

figure and the message of Jesus in the Gospel of Thomas are not interpreted within the framework of biblical traditions. It is also undisputed that many sayings of the Gospel of Thomas show a proximity to Platonic ideas (cf. the explanations on the differentiation between archetype and images, on the statements of immortality and pre-existence of the soul, on the transmigration of souls, etc.). It is again undisputed that in antiquity, a movement developed referring to both Platonic and Biblical ideas and which was labeled with the (extremely problematic) term 'Gnosis' or 'Gosticism'[23]. Leading representatives of Platonism, however, have again emphatically emphasized that Gnostic communities wrongly invoke Plato. So if the metaphor is used that 'Jesus meets Plato on the way to Gnosticism', then this illustrates the task that in regard to every single saying of the Gospel of Thomas it must be examined how close it is to Platonic and how close it is to 'Gnostic' ideas[24]. The latter depends on the reference texts to which the sayings of the Gospel of Thomas are related. If they are interpreted against the background of Platonic ideas, they can be understood as early approaches of a Christian-Platonic dialogue. If, on the other hand, gnostic conceptions are chosen as comparative variables, the result is a gnostic interpretation (cf. the explanations on Gos. Thom. 7; 19; 42; 49; 83; 84; 108 etc.)[25]. This can be impressively explained by the Coptic translation of the Gospel of Thomas found in the Nag Hammadi scriptures. This version is part of the second Codex. It is surrounded by further

---

23   Concerning these problems cf. M. Williams, Gnosticism, 29-54; 263f.; K. L. King, Gnosticism, 235f.

24   For a generally understandable introduction to the similarities and demarcations of Platonic and Gnostic ideas, I refer to my preliminary work in E. E. Popkes, Platonic Christianity, Chapter 2.4: The so-called 'Gnosis': a byway of the encounters between Platonism and early Christianity.

25   Accordingly, G. Theissen/A. Merz, Jesus, 54 spot a "Gnosis in statu nascendi". Regarding these debates cf. S. Gathercole, Thomas, 168ff.

texts, which show clear characteristics of a Gnostic world view[26]. This applies particularly to the so-called 'Apocryphon of John' (NHC II,1) and to the 'Gospel of Philip' (NHC II,3), which are placed immediately before and behind the Gospel of Thomas (NHC II,2). This can be interpreted as an indication of how those persons who formed this codex have interpreted the Gospel of Thomas. However, the message of earlier stages of the Gospel of Thomas cannot be explained in this way[27]. Instead: The sayings of the Gospel of Thomas can be interpreted against the background of Plato's theology. Within such a perspective they could be understood as early testimonies of a 'Platonic Christianity'. And the Gospel of Thomas understands Jesus as the founder of this movement.

2.8 Backgrounds of the Platonic Interpretation of the Figure and Message of Jesus in the Gospel of Thomas

The Platonic motifs of the Gospel of Thomas raise a question that can also be asked in relation to many other testimonies of early Christianity: what sources and ways of mediation were available to the author(s)? None of the words of Jesus in the Gospel of Thomas offers an explicit quotation from the *Corpus Platonicum* or even mentions the name Plato. There are also no references to contemporary discussions within schools of Middle-Platonism. However, this phenomenon is not extraordinary. It corresponds to many other testimonies, which were discovered among others in the codices of Nag Hammadi. How peculiar such mediations can be, can be explained by looking at the background of Gos. Thom.

---

26 For a generally understandable description of essential characteristics of so-called 'Gnosticism' see C. Markschies, Gnosis, 24f.

27 In this regard, I have modified an assessment of my earlier studies on the Gospel of Thomas, in which I have transferred the guidelines of an interpretation that can be developed on the basis of the structure of the second Nag Hammadi Codex to earlier stages of development of the Gospel of Thomas (cf. e.g. E. E. Popkes, Menschenbild, passim).

7. This saying refers to the motif of an 'inner man' (Plato, Resp. 588 c 1 - 589 a 8; for an interpretation, see Chapter 3). Plato uses the metaphor of a 'soul animal', which unites the essentials of different animals. It can hardly be denied that the lion metaphor present in Gos. Thom. 7 refers to those Platonic motifs. However, it remains debatable whether this background was known as such. This problem is even more evident when it is considered that this lion metaphor has been taken up in various Nag Hammadi writings. In NHC VI,5 actually, the text of Plato, Resp. 588a-589b has been paraphrased. However, not only is the translation very bad. It also documents that the person in charge obviously did not know that it was a text of the *Corpus Platonicum*[28].

Because of the background of such phenomena, it has sometimes been considered that the sayings of the Gospel of Thomas reflect a so-called 'vulgar Platonism' ("Vulgär-Platonismus"[29]). That term means, only a vague knowledge of Platonic thinking, without having perceived the texts of Plato or their interpretations. Also, the question of such an indirect mediation arises. One possible answer to this question may be found in the writings of Jewish-Hellenistic authors, such as e.g. Philo of Alexandria, Platonic approaches presented in the writings of the so-called 'Hermetism' as revelations of the mythical figure of Hermes Trismegistos, collections of proverbial wisdom such as the so-called 'Sentences of Sextus'[30] etc. Such routes of mediation are possible, but they remain merely more or less plausible speculations.

Nevertheless even if the sources of knowledge of Platonism can-

---

28   Cf. H.-M. Schenke, Platon, 356. According to J. Brashler, Plato, 325 this translation is "a disastrous failure" and "hopelessly confused".

29   Regarding the background of this term cf. H. Dörrie, Platonismus, 46f.

30   Cf. J. M. Robinson, LOGOI, 77-96; I. Miroshnikov, Plato, 25-44; S. Gathercole, Thomas, 168-175; W. Eisele, Sextus-Sprüche, passim; A. DeConick, Thomas, passim; E. Pagels, Gospel, passim. The phenomenon is concisely sumed up by S. J. Patterson, Plato, 183: "... what holds all these sphere of thought together – *Gnosis* (so-called), Philo, Hermeticism, Tatian – is their common interest in Plato."

not be clarified, the Gospel of Thomas can be understood as a part of the history of Platonism. On the one hand, just as many other testimonies of the ancient Mediterranean intellectual world the Gospel of Thomas documents the wide spread of Platonism. On the other hand, it can be understood as an innovative element in the history of Platonism: The interpretation of the figure and message of Jesus in the framework of platonic ideas is a testimony of a Platonic Christianity. And the Gospel of Thomas stylizes Jesus as the founder of Platonic Christianity.

> _Guiding assumption 2.10:_ The Gospel of Thomas embodies a new approach in the history of Platonism and early Christianity that can be named 'Platonic Christianity'.

2.9 The Gospel of Thomas, the Gospel of John and the 'Historical Jesus': a minor hint to a major problem

The preceding explanations lead to a question that is far more difficult to answer than it appears at first glance: Does the Gospel of Thomas have any relevance for the question of the so-called 'Historical Jesus'? In many contributions to the discourse this is basically denied. Not least because of this question, however, the Gospel of Thomas attracts a great deal of attention that reaches far beyond the boundaries of theology and church. Therefore, a field of discourse is to be opened in this chapter and will be continuously developed in the other volumes of the series 'Platonic Christianity'.

Since the beginning of historical-critical research regarding the history of early Christianity, one question has been formulated in many variations: Who was the person Jesus of Nazareth who inspired so many different interpretations of his life and his message? The extent to which the so-called 'Historical Jesus' or 'remembered Jesus' is even palpable is highly controversial[31]. These disputes already refer to the traditions handed down in the New Testament writings. An addition of the Gospel of Thomas potentiates the contentious questions considerably, because it conveys a completely different image of Jesus than is the case with the Synoptic and Johannine traditions[32]. Since the rediscovery of the Gospel of Thomas, it has been debated if it might be relevant to the question of the Historical Jesus. Many approaches to the discourse refer to traditions such as parables, beatitudes, individual motif traditions, etc. which connect the Gospel of Thomas with the Synoptic Gospels. Less attention, however, was given to the question of the importance that can be attached to those parallels, which associate the Gospel of Thomas with the Gospel of John. Also, it is already highly controversial whether the Gospel of John is relevant at all for the question of the Historical Jesus. Nevertheless, the fact that both works claim to go back to eyewitnesses, namely Thomas and the so-called beloved disciple, cannot be denied. In contrast to the synoptic gospels, both works claim to go back to eyewitnesses of Jesus, namely Thomas and the so-called 'beloved disciple' (cf. the explanations in step 2.6). This leads to a follow-up question: What is the reason for this claim?

---

31   For insights into the long and controversial history of research cf. T. Holmén/S. E. Porter, eds. Jesus, passim; J. Schröter/C. Jacobi, eds. Jesus-Handbuch, passim; B. Chilton/C. A. Evans, eds. Jesus, passim; G. Theissen/A. Merz, Jesus, 21-30; S. J. Patterson, Historical Jesus, 233-249. Espessially in regard to the position of the gospel of Thomas the assessment of S. J. Patterson, Way, 132 is indisputable: "Thomas has become an ideological flashpoint in the search for Christian origins".

32   For a sketch of the research debates most recently S. J. Patterson, Historical Jesus, 233-249. In regard to the peculiarity of the Gospel of Thomas within the history of early Christianity J. Schröter, Thomas, 506 states: "Die Einzigartigkeit des Thomasevangeliums innerhalb des Spektrums der frühchristlichen Literatur besteht ... darin, daß hier alte, mitunter bis zu Jesus selbst zurückreichende Traditionen aufgegriffen und durch die Zusammenstellung mit jüngeren Worten auf neue Weise interpretiert werden."

> *Guiding assumption 2.11:* The developments inspired by the
> early Jewish itinerant preacher Jesus of Nazareth can only be
> adequately understood by considering the Gospel of Thomas and
> the Gospel of John.

With the literary stylization of the so-called 'beloved disciple',
the Gospel of John documents a phenomenon that can often be
observed in extra-canonical writings of early Christianity: The le-
gitimacy of the views expressed is justified by the claim that they
go back to an alleged eyewitness of Jesus. In most cases, these
attempts can undoubtedly be understood as literary fictions. In
relation to the Gospel of John and the Gospel of Thomas, however, the possibility of the postulated eyewitnesseship must be considered more closely. Thus, for example, the following questions
arise: Why create the authors of these works images of the figure
and message Jesus that sometimes form direct contrast parallels?
Why do their images of Jesus differ from the picture of the itinerant preacher from Galilee as painted by synoptic traditions? Why
does the Gospel of Thomas not interpret the figure and message
of Jesus using biblical references? Does the name 'Thomas' stand
for a branch of early Christianity that detached the figure and
message of Jesus from its background within early Judaism and
placed it within a Platonic framework? Why does the author (or
authors) of the Gospel of Thomas take the trouble to describe
Jesus as the founder of a Platonic Christianity, when a Platonic
world view can also be conveyed completely independently of
that framework? In contrast to early Christianity, Platonic ideas
and schools were already widespread at that time.

Such questions in turn lead to a variation of the question with
which this chapter was introduced: Is the image of Jesus as described in the Gospel of Thomas at least partially linked to the
message of the Jewish itinerant preacher Jesus of Nazareth? Could
Jesus' message or parts of it have inspired a disciple like Thom-

as to a Platonic interpretation? This question will be explored, among others, in the fourth volume of the series 'Platonic Christianity'.

2.10 Secret Mosaics: Structure and Translation of the Gospel of Thomas

The following translations and interpretations often do not follow the order in which the individual words of Jesus are arranged in the Coptic version of the Gospel of Thomas. This is because of the fact that, as previously noted, the Gospel of Thomas sometimes resembles a disordered note box, put negatively. However, it can also – in a positiv sense – be understood as a collection of individual stones of a mosaic. The task is to bring the individual stones together to form meaningful images. Those can be described as 'hidden mosaics', since the sayings in their present arrangement often do not fit together thematically. If, however, they are arranged in the sense of individual thematic fields, coherent connections can be identified in themselves. The following interpretation of the Gospel of Thomas puts a possible design of such secret mosaics up for discussion. In particular, the translations and interpretations of these sayings form a coherent overall picture of a theological interpretation of the figure and message of Jesus.

Further methodological problems occur in regard to the translation of the Gospel of Thomas. The problems already begin with the question which version of the work is used as a point of reference. Studies of the materials and linguistic evidence suggest that the Coptic translation and the Greek fragments are relatively young[33]. A central question of the exegetical discussions is to what extent earlier textual stages can be reconstructed on the basis of these relatively recent testimonies. The Coptic translation also sometimes reveals grammatical errors that conceal the meaning of the sayings. In some cases, these ambiguities can be resolved by including the Greek fragments. Sometimes, however, it can only be speculated what the author of the saying originally wanted to express. Accordingly, for each individual saying it must be explained to what basis the translations and interpretations refer.

This can be illustrated by a problem for which a fundamental decision had to be made regarding the following translations. The individual sayings are usually introduced with a stereotypical formula. On the Coptic language level it is controversial whether this formula should be understood as a statement in the present ('Jesus says: ...') or in the past ('Jesus said: ...'). In the older Greek fragments, however, only the present form is used. In this sense, the Greek text form can be understood as a guideline for an interpretation of the Coptic translation[34]. However, with each individual saying it has to be explained how a modification of the Coptic text is justified. These explanations cannot be provided in the context of this study. In this regard, I refer once more to my preliminary work mentioned in the bibliography.

After giving basic information, the image of Jesus in the Gospel of Thomas as the founder of a Platonic Christianity can now be explained.

---

33 While the coptic translation and text version NHC II,2 was probably written in the first half of the fourth century (cf. S. Emmel, Witnesses, 33-49), the Greek fragments P.Oxy. 1; P.Oxy. 654; P.Oxy. 655 can be dated between the late second century and the middle of the third century (cf. L. Hurtado, Greek Fragments, 19-32; S. Gathercole, Thomas, 3ff; J. Schröter, Thomas, 488f.).

34 For this reason, the introductory formula is mostly translated in present tense. Exceptions to this premise are explicitly stated (see, inter alia, the comments on Gos. Thom. 12; 13).

3. "If you recognize yourselves ..." - Revelation by Self-Knowledge

The prologue and the first five words of Jesus already mention motifs that are of central importance for an understanding of the Gospel of Thomas. They can be described as follows:

a) There is a secret message of Jesus.
b) Thomas transmits through his gospel secret words of Jesus, which offer access to that secret message.
c) The readers of the Gospel of Thomas should seek and find the secret message of Jesus in the secret words of Jesus.
d) The seekers should not be confused by familiar authorities or patterns of thought, but rather engage in new ways of knowledge.
e) When they recognize themselves, they experience a revelation and a 'oneness' (*henosis*).
f) Whoever finds the secret message of Jesus will reign over the universe, will not 'taste death' and will find 'repose', the peace of perfection.

These motifs explain why the individual sayings of the Gospel of Thomas can be combined to form different mosaics. Different sayings must be assigned to each motif in order to develop its content. Strictly speaking, the order of reading is not relevant. Every path leads to the same goal.

The first words of the Gospel of Thomas already confront its readers with a provocative thesis: There is said to have been a message of Jesus which he did not communicate publicly and which is not immediately understandable.

Prologue
These are the secret sayings that the living Jesus spoke and Didymos Judas Thomas wrote them down.

The introductory statement is not taken for itself a peculiarity of the Gospel of Thomas. The biblical gospels also refer to such a message of Jesus (this especially applies to the 'mystery of the kingdom of God' implied in Mark 4:10-12). The Gospel of Thomas, however, emphasizes on the one hand to whom Jesus is said to have entrusted those secret words, namely Thomas. On the other hand, the readers are adressed in a way, without parallelism in the biblical gospels: They are encouraged to find the interpretation of that secret message. And whoever succeeds in this 'will not taste death'[35]. In other words, the secret words of Jesus give access to the knowledge of the immortality of one's own soul[36].

> *Gos. Thom. 1*
> And he said:
> > "Whoever finds the meaning of these sayings,
> > will not taste death."

The call of the first saying is unfolded in the second word of Jesus. Gos. Thom. 2 offers a rhetorically, artfully designed thesis for which there are only few analogies in New Testament traditions (cf. Matt 7:7-8; Luke 11:9-10; 1 Cor 4:8-9; 2 Tim 2:10-13). In the form of a *gradatio* the readers are invited to a continuous search for that interpretation.

---

35   This motif, which is repeated in various contexts (see the remarks on Gos. Thom. 18; 19), is slightly modified at the end of the Gospel of Thomas (Gos. Thom. 111:2: ' ... and who lives from the living one, will not see death.'). In the overall view of these texts, the phrase 'do not taste death' describes not less than "the Promise of Everlasting Life" (cf. A. Gagné, Thomas, 29).

36   The interpretation of the figure and the message of Jesus is conveyed within the Gospel of Thomas implies a thesis, as stated by S. J. Patterson, Way, 154: "One day everyone in Christendom would come to believe in Plato's immortal soul and look forward to the heavenly journey home. But in the first century, to find this familiar belief one must look to a very unfamiliar gospel, the Gospel of Thomas."

Gos. Thom. 2

(1) Jesus says:

"Whoever seeks shall not stop to seek,
until he finds.

(2)   And when he finds,
he will be astonished.

(3)   And when he is astonished,
he will begin to rule.

(4)   And when he has ruled,
he will find repose."[37]

With Gos. Thom. 2, readers are not only encouraged to do that search. They are also reminded of what could happen if they succeed: When they find that interpretation, they will be amazed and shaken. This gives rise to a new knowledge, which imparts a sovereign power to them. The goal of that development is that they find 'repose'. The so-called 'repose' is a central motif of the Gospel of Thomas, which is addressed in many sayings (Gos. Thom. 50; 51; 60; 90 etc.). It symbolizes the peaceful completion of human existence[38].

After the second saying encouraged the readers of the Gospel of Thomas, the third saying emphasizes that they must not be irritated during their search. Gos. Thom. 3 mentions for the first time people who are not directly addressed by the words of Jesus.

---

37   This form of the text corresponds to the Greek fragments (P.Oxy. 654:5-9) and traditions conveyed by the Egyptian theologian Clemens of Alexandria (Strom. II 45:5; V 96:3). The Coptic translation offers in regard to Gos. Thom. 2:4 the text: "And he will rule over the Universe." Remarkably, Clemens of Alexandria quotes this tradition several times and relates it to the Gospel of the Hebrews (cf. H.-G. Bethge, Thomas-Evangelium, 519; D. Lührmann/E. Schlarb, Fragmente, 48; S. Gathercole, Thomas, 198f.).

38   Regarding the contrast of the terms 'repose' and 'movement' in Platonic traditions and their affinities to the traditions of the Gospel of Thomas see S. J. Patterson, Plato, 200-204.

Gos. Thom. 3

(1) Jesus says:

>"If those who lead[39] you say to you:
>>'Behold, the kingdom is in the sky',
>
>the birds of the sky will precede you.

(2) If they say to you
>>'It is in the sea',
>
>the fish will precede you.

(3) Rather, the kingdom is inside of you
and outside of you.

(4) If you come to know yourselves,
then you will be known;
and you will realize,
that you are the children of the living father.

(5) But if you do not come to know yourselves,
then you exist in poverty and you are poverty."

The third saying conveys a new perspective. The first sayings of the Gospel of Thomas encourage their readers to search for the meaning of the secret words of Jesus. Gos. Thom. 3 mentions other persons who could hinder them during their search. This motif can be understood as a description of hierarchical structures that have developed in early Christianity. The readers of the Gospel of Thomas, however, should not be hindered in their search by those supposed authorities that claim to propagate appropriate interpretations of the Kingdom of the father. Rather, they should realize that they have access to that 'kingdom' everywhere, regardless of any ecclesiastical hierarchy. This motif will be further developed in a later context, especially in the contrast between James, the brother of Jesus, Jesus' supposedly orthodox disciples

---

39   The interpretation of the phrase οἱ ἕλκοντες (P.Oxy 654:10) caused many controversies, in particular with regard to the question if the phrase mirrors already established church structures. Concerning this debate cf. W. Eisele, Ziehen, 380-415, who interprets these words as a rephrasing of 'teaching'.

and Thomas (see the following explanations for Gos. Thom. 12; 13).

In Gos. Thom. 3:4-5 the goal of that search is considered from a new perspective. The final words of the third saying complement the motifs already introduced in the first and second saying by two aspects, which are further developed in different contexts. The readers should recognize themselves. They should realize that they are 'children of the living Father'. At first glance, this collection of motifs shows analogies to biblical gospels. At second glance, however, striking differences can be spotted. Gos. Thom. 3 documents an aspect that applies to almost every other saying of the Gospel of Thomas, which is the avoidance of the term 'God'. The combinations of motifs known from the biblical Gospels, such as 'Kingdom of God', 'God, the Father', 'Jesus, the Son of God', are almost completely absent in the Gospel of Thomas. The term 'God' is only mentioned in a critical manner (see Gos. Thom. 30). Instead, the sayings use the term father for God. This, in turn, is an analogy to the Gospel of John. And in this respect, again, the affinity and distance between the Gospel of Thomas and the Gospel of John can be seen. A central message of the figure of Jesus in the Gospel of John is that people *should become* children of God and children of the Father (John 1:12-13). The precondition for this is the faith that Jesus is the Son of God and Christ (John 20:30-31). A faith in Jesus as Christ has no relevance to the Gospel of Thomas. Rather, the Jesus of the Gospel of Thomas demands that people recognize themselves, as *already being* 'children of the Father'. A condition for this basic determination of their existence is not named[40].

After the exemplification of the precondition of their existences, the readers are confronted with an aim of their search by the immediately following saying Gos. Thom. 4:

---

40 Motifs of self-knowledge are already widespread in pre-Socratic traditions and are unfolded in Platonic concepts in various thematic contexts. For corresponding texts of the Gospel of Thomas cf. S. J. Patterson, Plato, 184-186.

Gos. Thom. 4

1) Jesus says:

"The man old in his days will not hesitate
to ask a child of seven days
about the place of life
- and he will live.

(2)   For there are many who are first
who will become last.
(and last first)[41].

(3)   And they will become one."

The fourth saying reveals a fact that can be observed in many of the words of Jesus in the Gospel of Thomas. On the one hand there are motifs that are known from the New Testament Gospels, e.g. the esteem for children (cf. Gos. Thom. 4:1 with Mark 9:37; 10:13-16 par.; Matt 18:1-4; 21:15-17) and the thesis that 'many first will be last' (cf. Gos. Thom. 4:2 with Mark 10:31; Matt 19:30). On the other hand, there are aspects that are not known from those contexts. In Gos. Thom. 4:1 there is a motif that seems puzzling at first glance: an old man, that is to say an experienced and educated person, lets himself be taught by a new-born infant about the 'place of life'. This paradox changes, however, when Gos. Thom. 4 is interpreted against the background of many other sayings of the Gospel of Thomas, which convey the idea of a preexistence and transmigration of souls (cf. the following explanations on Gos. Thom. 18; 19; 49; 50; 83; 84 etc.).

Special attention should also be paid to the motif of 'becoming one', which is present in the final statement of Gos. Thom. 4. In the context of Gos. Thom. 4 this detail is not explained in detail. However, it is unfolded in many other sayings of the Gospel of Thomas and thus stylized to a central theme of the work (cf. the

---

41   The second part of the statement of Gos. Thom. 4:2 is conveyed within the Greek fragments only (P.Oxy 654:21-27).

explanations to Gos. Thom. 13; 16; 22; 49; 75; 108 etc.).

The prologue and the first four sayings of the Gospel of Thomas thus already expose central motifs that readers should pay attention to. In the following explanations the chronological order of the sayings will be left. Instead, it will be focused on those sayings, which are important for a deeper understanding of the already described topics. This can be explained by the contrast of 'seeking' and 'finding'. For example, Gos. Thom. 92:1 also puts forward the thesis that those who do not allow themselves to be confused in their search for the interpretation of Jesus' secret message will find that interpretation[42]. However, a motive is added which was only indirectly recognizable in those first words of Jesus, namely the distinction between a message, which Jesus previously did not want to communicate but now wants to communicate (Gos. Thom. 92:2).

Gos. Thom. 92
(1) Jesus says:
    "Seek and you will find.
(2)   But the things you asked me about in former times,
       and what I did not tell you then,
       I want to tell you now,
       but you do not seek for it."

There are analogies with various testimonies of early Christianity, when considering the distinction of different stages of a mediation of the message of Jesus. This phenomenon reflects different strategies to legitimize a theological concept. And in this respect, again, a remarkable affinity and distance between the Gospel of Thomas and the Gospel of John can be observed.

A peculiarity of the Gospel of Thomas is that it places the mes-

---

42   The motif of searching shows an analogy to Matt 7:7-11//Luke 11:11-13 (cf. U.-K. Plisch, Thomasevangelium, 220f.).

sage of Jesus in a framework of interpretation that is fundamentally different from many other early Christian concepts. Already in Gos. Thom. 3:1-2 it was emphasized that readers should not let themselves be confused by people who claim to be their leaders. They would propagate an understanding of the message of Jesus that will not lead to having insight into the secret message of Jesus. Such problematic understandings are, inter alia, addressed in Gos. Thom. 18; 19; 51; 52; 53; 113. And again, the following consideration does not correspond to the order in which the sayings occur in the Coptic translation of the Gospel of Thomas. Instead, the sayings will be arranged according to their content.

Gos. Thom 52 is focusing an understading of the figure and message of Jesus, which is – according to Gospel of Thomas – a misconception. According to this saying, the secret message of Jesus should not be searched in the context of prophecies, conveyed through the Jewish bible and early Jewish traditions:

> *Gos. Thom. 52*
> (1) His disciples said to him:
> > "Twenty-four prophets have spoken in Israel,
> > and all have spoken about you.'
> (2) He said to them:
> > "You have dismissed the living one from youselves,
> > and you have begun to speak of the dead."

Such a dissociation from the message of the Jewish bible fundamentally distinguishes the Gospel of Thomas from most of the testimonies that can be found within the New Testaments writings. Because of this, it is hardly surprising that in the immediately following saying a problem is brought into focus, which was of great importance for the development of early Christianity.

Gos. Thom. 53

(1) His disciples said to him:
   "Is circumcision helpful or not?"

(2) He said to them:
   "If it were helpful,
   their father would beget them already circumcised from
   their mother.

(3)   Rather, the true circumcision in the spirit
   is helpful in every way."

According to Gos. Thom. 53 Jesus had been asked by his disciples whether circumcision matters or not. Such a question has no analogy within the biblical Gospels. Instead, Gos. Thom. 53 reflects questions that occur in different early Christian communities which address the importance of the observance of the Jewish law. The answer of the gospel of Thomas is rigorous in this respect: it is meaningless and can even be problematic (cf. Gos. Thom. 6/14). Also other ideas, which some groups of early Christianity have in common with early Jewish expectations, are dismissed as fundamentally wrong. This applies above all to the traditional expectation of a resurrection of the dead, the dawn of a new world and the associated expectations of a kingdom of God (cf. Gos. Thom. 18; 51; 113)[43]:

---

43 Cf. N. T. Wright, Resurrection, 536: "The saying expressly rejects the early Christian expectation of a final divine act in history producing new heavens and new earth."

Gos. Thom. 51

(1) His disciples said to him:

"When will the repose (resurrection)[44]

of the dead come about?

And when will the new world come?"

(2) He said to them:

"That what you are waiting for,

has already come, but you do not recognize it."

Gos. Thom. 113

(1) His disciples said to him:

"When will the kingdom come?"

(2) (Jesus says)[45]:

"It will not come, when you look for it.

(3)   It will not be said:

'Look, here!' or 'Look, there!'

(4)   Instead of that, the kingdom of the Father is spread

out upon the earth,

and human beings do not see it."

However, it should not only be asked which expectations in the Gospel of Thomas are rejected. It also needs to be asked what should be the expectations alternatively. This is already evident in one of the first sayings of the work.

---

44   The coptic translation uses the term 'repose' (*anapausis*) that was discussed immediately prior to Gos. Thom. 50. For this reason, it is possible that Gos. Thom. 51 originally used the phonetically similar term 'resurrection' (*anastasis*) that was confused during the process of translation (cf. H.-G. Bethge, Thomas-Evangelium, 532).

45   Even though the text does not explicitly identify Gos. Thom. 113:2-3 as an answer of Jesus, it is undisputed that these words are attributed to Jesus (a comparable phenomenon occurs in the transition from Gos. Thom. 43:1 to Gos. Thom. 43:2-3).

Gos. Thom. 5

(1) Jesus says:

"Recognize what is in front of your eyes,

and that what is hidden from you,

will be revealed to you.

(2)   Because there is nothing hidden

that will not be revealed."[46]

The Jesus of the Gospel of Thomas requests his disciples to recognize what is 'before their eyes'. This may raise the question in
the readers of the Gospel of Thomas what could be meant by the
statement 'before your face'. An explicit answer to this question
does not occur in the context of Gos. Thom. 5. Instead, in the following saying Gos. Thom. 6:5, as well as Gos. Thom. 5:2, it is emphasized once again that all hidden things will be revealed. However, the perspective can be changed if other sayings are included
into the interpretation. Such a perspective reveals new mosaics of
textual formations that are related in content and terminology.
This is particularly evident in the case of the sayings Gos. Thom.
56; 80 and Gos. Thom. 87; 112[47].

---

46   A. Luijendijk, Resurrection, 272-296 shows the immediate relation of the
topics 'conceal'/'reveal' and 'bury'/'rise' and how they can also be relevant for
the understanding of resurrection in the Gospel of Thomas. This is an example of how the design of the Gospel of Thomas, as a collection of individual
sayings, reveals those 'hidden mosaics' that were put up for discussion as the
guiding structure of the collection (see chapter 2.10). The sequence of reading
described above followed the terms 'seek'/'find' that were brought into focus at
the first sayings. If one had not continued the reading of Gos. Thom. 4 with the
thematically corresponding saying Gos. Thom. 92, the reading of Gos. Thom. 5
would have opened up a different topic that would aim at sayings such as Gos.
Thom. 51 or Gos. Thom. 18; 19 etc.

47   For the platonic analogies to the concepts of 'soul', 'body' and 'cosmos'
unfolded in Gos. Thom. 56; 80/87/112, cf. I. Miroshnikov, Plato, 45-90; S. J.
Patterson, Plato, 186-190.

Gos. Thom. 56
(1) Jesus says:
    "Whoever has recognized the world,
    has found a corpse.
(2)   And whoever has found a corpse,
    the world is unworthy to him."

Gos. Thom. 80
(1) Jesus says:
    "Whoever has recognized the world,
    has found the body.
(2)   But whoever has found the body,
    the world is unworthy to him."

The analogies of these sayings are obvious. Often they were understood as doublets, which were handed down twice by mistake. However, such an assessment, in my opinion, confounds the concerns of both texts. In addition to minimal syntactic differences, a shift of emphasis can be identified that is remarkable in terms of language and content. Both sayings bring into focus the knowledge of the cosmos (Gos. Thom. 56:1a; 80:1a) and the consequences of this realization: When someone understands the world, the world will appear 'unworthy' to him (Gos. Thom. 56:2b; 80:2b)[48]. However, there are differences regarding the point of reference. While Gos. Thom. 56:1b.2a speaks of a 'corpse', Gos. Thom. 56:1b.2a speaks of the 'body'. The importance of this difference is only recognizable within the Greek and Coptic language – or more precisely: audible. The Greek and Coptic terms πτῶμα/ⲡⲧⲱⲙⲁ (*toma*) and σῶμα/ⲥⲱⲙⲁ (*soma*) can only be distinguished by their first letters. When these two sayings are re-

---

48 A further variation of this motif occurs in Gos. Thom. 111:3. Nevertheless, as in Gos. Thom. 61:5, it seems to be a comment that has been included in an already existing text (Gos. Thom. 111:3: "Does not Jesus say, 'Whoever has found himself, the world is not worthy of him.'").

cited one after the other, the phonetic proximity of the words 'body' and 'corpse' rhymes. When these statements are continually repeated like a prayer, it expresses a specific understanding of human existence: a body is a 'corpse', a 'corpse' is a 'body'.

These statements open up a further indication in what sense the message of Jesus is interpreted in the Gospel of Thomas, namely in the sense of Platonism. That the body should be a corpse is directly reminiscent of the statements of Plato in which the mortal body is called the 'grave' or 'prison' of the immortal soul (see Plato Phaed. 62b, Gorg. 493a, Phaedr. 250c). Plato also communicates this with a phonetic play of words: the Greek term for 'body' (σῶμα/soma) is also very close to the term 'grave' (σῆμα/sema).

With this easily recognizable analogy of Gos. Thom. 56 to a platonic motif, however, a fundamental question becomes important, which will accompany all further considerations of the sayings of the Gospel of Thomas: to which extent can the Gospel of Thomas be understood as a testimony of a Platonic Christianity or as a testimony of a Gnostic interpretation of Platonism? [49] However, the delimitation of Platonic and Gnostic ideas has not only a fundamental meaning for the interpretation of the Gospel of Thomas, but for all the sub-volumes of the series 'Platonic Christianity'. It is precisely at these borderlines that those 'hidden discourses' emerge which are revived by the underlying historical-critical and discourse-analytical method[50]. In this regard, it is helpful to refer back to the metapher explained above, according to which 'Jesus meets Plato on the way to Gnosticism' (see chapter 2.7). According to that metaphor, the position of every single saying of the Gospel of Thomas has to be debated – namely its positions

---

49   The critique of 'cosmos' and 'body' in Gos. Thom. 56; 80; 87; 112 is stated accurately by S. Gathercole, Thomas, 428: "These characterisations of the world as spiritually dead are the two most anti-cosmic sayings in Thomas, since 'death' is perhaps the most negatively valued spiritual state."

50   Regarding the topic of 'hidden discourses' I refer to my preliminary studies in E. E. Popkes, Platonic Christianity, Chapter 3.

on the long path of the developments of Platonism and 'gnostic' interpretations of Platonism.

The difficulties of these approaches can be demonstrated in regard to the further interpretation of Gos. Thom. 56; 80. According to the concept of hidden mosaics, a reader of the Gospel of Thomas should search for other sayings which adress the relationship between the cosmos and the body. A new constellation of a mosaic arises by the considerations of Gos. Thom. 87; 112 and Gos. Thom. 7:

Gos. Thom. 87
(1) Jesus says:
"Misery is the body,
that depands on a body.
(2)   misery is the soul,
that depands on these two."

Gos. Thom. 112
(1) Jesus says:
"Woe to the flesh
that depends on the soul.
(2)   Woe to the soul,
that depends on the flesh."

Gos. Thom. 7
(1) Jesus says:
"Blessed is the lion,
that a human being will eat.
And the lion will be human being.
(2)   And cursed is the human being
that the lion will eat.

And the human being will be lion."[51]

All three sayings cloesy resemble to Platonic ideas. However, they can also be interpreted in the framework of Gnostic systems. As an example, this is evident in Gos. Thom. 7. This saying is based on a metaphor with which Plato illustrates his idea of an 'inner man'[52]. For this purpose, he uses the metaphor of a 'soul animal' to unite different animals and their attributes (Plato, Resp. 588 c 1 – 589 a 8f.). The 'inner man' represents the mind-oriented dimension of the soul, which for Plato is immortal and imperishable. The metaphor of the lion stands for the physical-affective orientation of human existence, which is to be controlled by a mental-spiritual growth process. If this process does not succeed, human beings will be devoured by their desires, as by a lion[53]. In this respect, Gos. Thom. 7 also corresponds to Gos. Thom. 87. According to this saying the soul of a human being must not be dominated by bodily desires.

The analogies between Gos. Thom. 87; 112 and Gos. Thom. 56; 80 are again obvious. And even within these sayings a terminological difference can be observed, which is hardly accidental. Just as before in Gos. Thom. 80, the physical dimension of human existence is described in Gos. Thom. 87:1 by the term 'body'. On

---

51   In the Coptic text version, Gos. Thom. 7:2 contains a text that is almost similar to Gos. Thom. 7:1 and thus makes no sense. For this reason, a translation error is usually postulated and corrected. Regarding these debates cf. I. Miroshnikov, Plato, 188f.

52   The analogies between Gos. Thom. 7 and platonic ideas are indisputable. Open to discussion are, however, the precise backgrounds of this saying. Cf. H. M. Jackson, Lion, passim; I. Miroshnikov, Plato, 188-220; L. Roig Lanzillotta, Logion 7, 116-132.

53   The intention of Plato's metaphor is summarizd aptly by B. Fröhlich, Selbsterkenntnis, 410: "In dem ... Bild des 'Seelentiers' ... wird der begehrende Seelenteil (ἐπιθυμητικόν) mit einem bunten und vielköpfigen Tier verglichen und das eifrige, mutartige Vermögen (θυμικόν) mit einem Löwen. Die Vernunftseele (λογιστικόν) hingegen bestimmt Platon als Mensch ... noch präziser: als 'innerer Mensch' (ὁ ἐντός ἄνθρωπος) des Menschen ..., da ja der Mensch zuvor als das aus allen Kräften Zusammengewachsene bezeichnet worden war."

the contrary, the term 'flesh' is used in Gos. Thom. 112. This detail is remarkable: the relation of the terms 'body' and 'flesh' are reflected in different early Christian traditions, not least in controversies regarding different understandings of resurrection (cf. 1 Cor 15:35-49). With these sayings, a topic is introduced that drew a great attention in the history of early Christianity. According to the terminology, which is used in all volumes of the series 'Platonic Christianity', this topic can be described as follows: it is about the history of the confrontation of contrary understandings of human existences and eschatological hopes, which coincide with the discourse positions 'bodily resurrection of the Dead' and 'immortality of the soul'. Or to put it as a question: what are those aspects of human existence that are referred to by the terms 'body', 'soul', 'spirit' and 'mind'? And what happens to these aspects of human existence when the body dies?

Gos. Thom. 87 gives a further indication what is of fundamental importance for an understanding of the Gospel of Thomas: according to the Gospel of Thomas, the immortal soul exists only temporarily in a body and in this world. In this sense, a saying of the Gospel of Thomas which is at first glance difficult to understand, can be interpreted relatively easily:

Gos. Thom. 42
Jesus says: "Become passersby."

Gos. Thom. 42 is by far the shortest saying of the Gospel of Thomas. It confronts its readers with the demand to become 'passersby'. Against the background of the biblical Gospels, such a demand may seem strange. The situation is different, however, if one interprets Gos. Thom. 42 against the background of the short formula '... from here to there ... ', which expresses the 'core of all

Platonism'[54] in a compressed form. The first part of this formula can be interpreted easily against the background of the texts considered so far: 'here' marks the bodily existences within this cosmos. Or, to put it in the words of Gos. Thom. 5:1: it is what is immediately visible to the seekers, and thus what is 'before their face'. However, one could ask what 'there' denotes in the sense of that 'short formula of all Platonism'? According to the Gospel of Thomas, the answer to this question is clear and univocal: it is the heavenly home from which human beings come. It is the 'light that has arisen out of itself' (Gos. Thom. 50:1), it is the kingdom of the Father (Gos. Thom. 49:1), it is Jesus as one incarnation of that omnipresent light from which everything has risen and towards which everything strives (Gos. Thom. 77).

However, before these features of the Gospel of Thomas will be unfolded, it is important to consider other aspects that are relevant to the understanding of the topics of self-knowledge and revelation. The starting point for the sketched explanation of the sayings Gos. Thom. 42; 56; 80; 87; 111; 112 was the saying Gos. Thom 5:1 and the question what the phrase 'before their face' meant. In the manner described, that phrase characterizes the material-physical constitution of human existence, which is to be distinguished from a spiritual dimension. However, there is another aspect of Gos. Thom. 5:1 that needs to be considered. The phrase '... and that what is hidden from you will be revealed to you' contains an accent that differs from similar-sounding formulations. At first glance, this difference seems to be insignificant. A revelation of hidden things is also mentioned in other tradi-

---

54 This phrase is referring T. Szlezák, Seele, 32f.: "Geben wir der Vernunftseele in uns die Herrschaft, so werden wir durch sie von hier nach dort gezogen – so lautet die platonische Kurzformel für alles, wofür seine Philosophie steht: für die Bewegung von der Werdewelt zur Welt der unvergänglichen Ideen, vom Sinnlichen zum Intelligiblen: ἐντένδε ἐκεῖσε. Das ist der Kern von allem Platonismus, durch Platon selbst, einem Meister der Sprache, in ganze zwei Worte gefasst." Regarding a detailed interpretation of this topic cf. B. T. Schur, Philosophiebegriff, passim; E. E. Popkes, Theology of Plato, Chapter 3 and 4.

tions concerning the message of Jesus or in the Pauline letters (cf. Mark 4:22; Luke 8:17-18; 12: 2-3, Matt 10:26; Rom 2:16; 1 Cor 2:6-16; 4:5 etc.). A peculiarity of Gos. Thom. 5, however, is the relationship between knowledge and revelation. As in various other sayings of the Gospel of Thomas, a revelation is designated as the consequence of that search for knowledge (cf. the preceding interpretation of Gos. Thom. 92). Jesus and his message of are not understood as a revelation of God to believe in. The message of Jesus is rather that he challenges people to gain the knowledge of who he is and who they are. The differences between this concept and other early Christian understandings of faith and knowledge becomes evident when one compares GosThom 91 and GosThom 17.

Gos. Thom. 91
(1) They said to him:
>   "Tell us who you are that we may believe in you."
(2) He said to them:
>   "You examine the appearance of the sky
>   and the earth,
>   but you have not recognized the one
>   who stands before you,
>   nor do you know to benefit this special occasion."

Gos. Thom. 17
Jesus says:
>   "I will give you,
>   what no eye has seen
>   and no ear has heard
>   and no hand has touched
>   and what has not arisen in the human mind."

Gos. Thom. 91 is structured like many other sayings of the Gospel of Thomas. The disciples are asking a question. However, Jesus' response documents that the question itself is wrong. Gos. Thom. 91:1 describes the motif of having faith in Jesus central to many early Christian traditions. However, the Jesus of the Gospel of Thomas does not want his disciples to believe in him. They shall recognize him (Gos. Thom. 91:2) and the knowledge of Jesus ultimately leads to self-knowledge. However, what is a crucial element of this cognitive process is brought up by Gos. Thom. 17: the Jesus of the Gospel of Thomas opens up a new approach to self-knowledge. His mediator position is that this approach has so far been perceived by 'no eye, no ear and no hand' – that is, by the media of human cognitive ability.

This motif is remarkable in several ways. It is an impressive example of the way in which the figure and message of Jesus is interpreted in a Platonic manner. In the sense of the theology and the anthropology of Plato, the mind, and thus the immortal aspect of the human soul, is in direct contact with God[55]. This aspect would therefore not be an innovative thesis in the context of a Platonic school. However, the specific Platonic-Christian approach consists of three aspects: On the one hand, Jesus is interpreted as an earthly presence of that principle of creation from which the whole creation originates and for which the entire creation strives (cf. chapter 5: "I am the light ..." – The Origin and the Perfection of the Creation). On the other hand, a central message of the Gospel of Thomas is that all human beings should become a 'person of light', who in turn enlightens the world (cf. chapter 6: "... and it enlightens the whole world." – The divine light within human beings). And this process of development takes place in those human beings who become like Jesus or that light (cf. chapter 4: "... you will become like me." – Oneness with Jesus).

---

55   See, i.a. Plato Tim. 90 a 2-6: "The most important form of soul in us, however, we must think as follows, namely, that God has given each of us as a guardian spirit; we assert that she dwells in the highest part of our body and raises us from the earth to our relationship in heaven, since we are not an earthly, but a heavenly plant." (ὄντας φυτὸν οὐκ ἔγγειον ἀλλὰ οὐράνιον).

> *Guiding assumption 2.12:* The Gospel of Thomas conveys central ideas of Platonism as a message of Jesus, above all the ideas of the immortality of the soul, of becoming like God, of the differentiation between immortal archetypes and mortal images and of the knowledge of the 'true light'.

A further perspective on the importance of self-knowledge is focused in the two sayings Gos. Thom. 12; 13, which are directly related with each other. In this context, an aspect is unfolded that has already been suggested in Gos. Thom. 3:1-2: whoever is searching for the secret message of Jesus must not be irritated by persons who claim to have a leading role. This proclamation remains indefinite in the context of Gos.Thom 3 and is focused more precisely in Gos. Thom. 12; 13. Both sayings are of high relevance to the question in which historical contexts the Gospel of Thomas was shaped and could have been read.

Gos. Thom. 12
(1) The disciples said to Jesus[56]:
   "We know that you will depart from us.
   Who will be eminent among us?
(2) Jesus said to them:
   "No matter where you came from,
   you shall go to James the Just,
   the one for whom heaven and earth
   came into being."

---

56   For reasons of grammar and content it is more plausible to interpret Gos. Thom. 12; 13 as well as Gos. Thom. 79; 99; 104 as narratives of the past (in contrast to the initial considerations in Chapter 2.10).

The central figure of Gos. Thom. 12 is James, the brother of Je-sus[57]. The authority this figure had in early Christianity is already documented in various New Testament writings. The reason why James was able to obtain this authority is not explained within biblical testimonies. Even Paul mentions James as the authori-ty of the Jerusalem community, without having to explain this fact to his readers in more detail (Gal 1:19; 2:11-12). The letter of James also represents a resolute self-claim that could not be explained without a special position of the brother of Jesus. The same applies to the mention of James in Acts, in which he is rep-resented as a central authority (cf. Acts 12:17; 15:13-21; 21:18-36). However, if one wants to understand how these developments came about, non-Canonical writings must be included into the discussion. Of particular importance are the testimonies of the so-called 'Jewish Christianity', that is to say, those forms of Chris-tian communities that have continued to practice essential char-acteristics of Jewish religiousness. The high authority of James within Jewish Christianity is documented clearly in the Gospel of the Hebrews, in the so-called 'Pseudo-Clementine Writings' etc. Like Eusebius of Caesarea (about 260-330 CE), the author of the first church history, these testimonies are in agreement that Je-sus himself named his brother as his successor. This idea is also handed down as an explicit instruction of Jesus in Gos. Thom. 12. But even if the Gospel of Thomas grants a special status to the brother of Jesus, this cannot be taken as an indication that the Gospel of Thomas originated from Jewish Christian circles. On the one hand, the Jewish backgrounds of early Christianity are viewed critically (cf. the preceding explanations on Gos. Thom. 52, 53 etc.). On the other hand, the immediately following say-ing Gos. Thom. 13 illustrates that not James, but Thomas is the central authority for those disciples, who search for the secret

---

57   On the multifaceted spectrum of early Christian traditions on the brother of Jesus cf. R. Bauckham, James, 55-95; W. Pratscher, Jakobus, passim; M. Hengel, Jakobus, passim; J. Painter, James, passim etc.

message of Jesus[58].

Beside the prologue, Gos. Thom. 13 is the only saying in which Thomas is mentioned again. It can be understood as a narrative illustration of Gos. Thom. 62, according to which Jesus entrusts his mysteries only to those who have shown themself worthy to do so. This leads to the question of what is the condition for Jesus entrusting his mysteries to a particular person. With that in mind, it is certainly no coincidence that Gos. Thom. 13 is the only saying that stylizes a longer dialogue between Jesus and his disciples.

Gos. Thom. 13

(1) Jesus said to his disciples:

"Compare me and tell me whom I resemble."

(2) Simon Peter said to him:

"You are like a just angel."

(3) Matthew said to him:

"You are like a wise philosopher."

(4) Thomas said to him:

"Teacher, my mouth is absolutely unable to say whom you are like!"

(5) Jesus said:

"I am not your teacher!

Because you have drunk,

You have become intoxicated by the bubbling spring, which I have measured out."

(6) And he took him (and) withdrew (and) (and) said three words to him.

---

58 Accordingly, J. Schröter, Thomas, 506 notes regarding the relationship of Gos. Thom. 12 and Gos. Thom. 13: "Diese Abfolge ist nicht auf eine Abwertung des Jakobus, sondern auf eine Herausstellung der jeweiligen Funktion von Thomas und Jakobus zurückzuführen: An Jakobus werden die Jünger für die Zeit der Abwesenheit Jesu verwiesen, Thomas dagegen gilt als derjenige, der die verborgene Lehre Jesu bereits empfangen hat und dadurch zu deren Tradent und zugleich zum Exempel für den Weg der Erlösung geworden ist."

(7) But when Thomas returned to his companions,
    they asked him:
        "What did Jesus tell you?"
(8) Thomas said to them:
        "If I tell you one of the words, he told me
        you will pick up stones (and) throw them at me,
        and fire will come out of the stones
        (and) burn you up."

The short, but complex scenery is a reminiscent of the so-called 'confession of Peter'. According to Mark 8:27-30, Peter was the first person among the disciples of Jesus to have explicitly stated that they considered Jesus as the expected Messiah (see Mark 8:27-30 par.). However, the term 'Messiah' is not mentioned in Gos. Thom. 13 and throughout the rest of the Gospel of Thomas. In contrast, Jesus is first compared to an angel or a philosopher. These aspects in turn reveal what is evident in many of the other sayings of the Gospel of Thomas: Jesus' words and deeds are not interpreted in the context of biblical expectations.

However, the actual intention of Gos. Thom. 13 becomes clear in the narrative of a dialogue between Jesus and Thomas. Thomas is said to have argued that he does not dare to say who Jesus is in his opinion. Then Jesus confronts him with the thesis that he is not (or no longer) his teacher. This assessment is justified by the following motif: Thomas drank from the spring that Jesus made accessible. Jesus separates Thomas from his other disciples and entrusts him with three secret words. According to the narration, the other disciples want to hear from Thomas what Jesus had told him. However, the dialogue implies the thesis that those words would lead to the persecution of Thomas. The rest of Jesus' disciples would mistake them for a heresy justifying a stoning of Thomas.

Special attention should be given to the following aspects: According to the narrative of Gos. Thom. 13, the content of those three secret words is not named. For the readers of the Gospel, however, there are ways to interpret those three words. For example, it would be possible that Jesus has called himself a divine figure. On the one hand, this would correspond to the statement of Gos. Thom. 77, in which Jesus is designated as the origin and destination of all existence (for further details, see Chapter 4). On the other hand, the deification of a human figure in the context of a Jewish religiosity would be a presumptuous judgment, which various biblical narratives of the words and deeds of Jesus also reflect. Especially traditions regarding the trial of Jesus, which took place before the Sanhedrin emphasize this view. On the part of the highest Jewish judiciary, the real reason for condemning Jesus was his self-esteem to have a special relationship with God (see Mark 14: 61-62//Matt 26:63-66//Luke 22:66-71). Likewise, it is highlighted in various contexts that Jesus claimed to perform exorcisms by the power of God (Luke 11:20//Matt. 12:28). This self-affirmation led supporters of contemporary Judaism to believe that Jesus himself was demonically possessed (Mark 3:22//Luke 11:15//Matt 12:24).

However, such a self-claim is most clearly conveyed by an image of Jesus that is elaborated within the Gospel of John. The Johannine Jesus claims for himself what was said in the prologue to the Gospel concerning the relationship between God and the Logos (cf. John 1:1-3, especially V 1c: καὶ θεὸς ἦν ὁ λόγος [" ... and God was the word" .]). Within the narration of the Fourth Gospel, the Johannine Jesus confronts his interlocutors with the thesis that he is one with God, his Father (John 10:30: ἐγὼ καὶ ὁ πατὴρ ἕν ἐσμεν). The reaction of the interlocutors would have been legitimate in the sense of a Jewish religiosity: they want to stone Jesus (John 10:31). In his farewell speech to his disciples, Jesus emphatically repeats this self-claim: whoever sees him would see his father (John 14:6-9). And the Gospel of John finally finds its culmination in the confession of Thomas that Jesus is 'his Lord and his God' (John 20:28b: ὁ κύριός μου καὶ ὁ θεός μου). A deification of Jesus is thus no longer a stumbling block in the context of advanced stages of development within early Christian traditions. But what would legitimate – in the sense of Gos. Thom. 13:8 – a death sentence for a statement that Jesus should have just entrusted to Thomas? To my opinion, the Gospel of Thomas offers a possible answer to this question that can be explained easily in comparison: the Gospel of Thomas, like the Gospel of John, presupposes the deification of Jesus. However, in contrast to the Gospel of John, it finds its real culmination in the motif of the deification of all human beings. In other words: the central message of the Gospel of Thomas is thus the motif of 'becoming one with Jesus' (see Gos. Thom. 108).

Against such a background, even those three words, entrusted to Thomas, can be interpreted easily. In the sense of the supposedly original language of the Gospel of Thomas, these may simply be: ἡμεῖς ἕν ἐσμεν ('We are one.'). This motif will be considered in the next chapter.

4. "… you will become like me." – Oneness with Jesus

Formally considered, Gos. Thom. 108 is one of the shorter sayings of the Gospel of Thomas. With regards to its content, however, it has a significance that can hardly be overestimated – especially for the interpretation that is put up for discussion with this book.

> *Gos. Thom. 108*
> (1) Jesus says:
>   "Whoever will drink from my mouth,
>   will become like me.
> (2)   I myself will become he.
> (3)   And the hidden things will be revealed to him."

The Jesus of the Gospel of Thomas confronts his readers with a thesis that is fundamentally different from the various biblical images of Jesus: Whoever drinks from the mouth of Jesus will become like him (Gos. Thom. 108:1). Jesus himself will become this person (Gos. Thom. 108:2)[59]. This topic has a central meaning for the search of the secret message of Jesus to which the readers of the Gospel of Thomas were already challenged by the first sayings: the hidden things will be revealed to those who find the secret message of Jesus and become one with him (Gos. Thom. 1; 108,3).

The motif of becoming one with Jesus has experienced interpretations that sometimes differ significantly. On several occasions, the thesis has been formulated that this is actually only a variation of those ethical appeals that are also known from biblical gospels: if the disciples of Jesus behave similar to their teacher, they would personify his will and commandments. However, such an interpretation does not correspond to other central sayings of

---

[59]   Accordingly, U.-K. Plisch, Thomasevangelium, 249 emphazises that Gos. Thom. 108 can be understood as one of the most mystical sayings of the Gospel of Thomas.

the Gospel of Thomas, which pay only a relatively small amount of attention to the ethical dimensions of the message of Jesus. Likewise, it was considered whether Gos. Thom. 108 is similar to a motif Paul mentions in various context, namely, the motif that the community of believers will be 'one in Christ' (Gal. 3:28b) and embody the presence of Christ (cf. Gal 2:20 and the motif of the 'body of Christ' in 1 Cor 12:27)[60]. In this regard, however, it should be noted that terms such as 'faith' and 'Christ' are not relevant to the sayings of the Gospel of Thomas (such references are also discussed in the context of the motif of 'becoming one' in chapter 7).

Gos. Thom. 108, however, speaks of an oneness of being between Jesus and his disciples, which is formed step by step. So one can ask what the figure of Jesus is held for in the Gospel of Thomas. It has been postulated on several occasions that the sayings of this testimony give the impression that Jesus acted like a teacher of wisdom. Such an assessment is not fundamentally wrong, but it falls short. Central texts of the Gospel of Thomas present Jesus as a divine figure (cf. the interpretion of Gos. Thom. 77 in chapter 5). Against the background of these references, the motif of becoming one with Jesus can be understood as an early Christian interpretation of a central theme of Plato's theology and anthropology, and indeed as an interpretation of the motif of becoming like God (Plato, Theaet. 176 b 1-3)[61].

Before this matter is explained in the following chapter, one aspect has to be considered which has come to light in various instances

---

60   Cf. R. Nordsieck, Thomasevangelium, 370; T. Zöckler, Lehren, 245f.; W. Eisele, Thomas, 67 etc.

61   Similarly, S. Gathercole, Thomas, 158, who at the same time emphasizes parallels to other extra-canonical testimonies of early Christianity, summarizes: „The degree of assimilation here is strong, reflecting more than a Pauline imagery of being *in* Christ, and closer to the kind of 'unitive mysticism' or ὁμοίωσις θεῷ in the strong sense in the *Gospel of Eve* or the *Gospel of Philipp*." For a sketch of other early Christian images of the Platonic motif of becoming like God cf. G. H. van Kooten, Anthropology, 124-180.

in the preceding explanations: the most striking parallels to the sketched features of the Gospel of Thomas occur in the Gospel of John. The Jesus of John's gospel confronts his disciples with the statement that he and his father are one (John 10:30). Whoever sees Jesus, sees the father (John 14:9). They will realize that he and the father dwell in their fellowship (John 14:20). Similarly, the author of the Fourth Gospel lets Jesus pray to his Father that they will be one with those who believe in them (John 17:20-21). And in this regard the same question arises once more: to which extent have the Gospel of Thomas and the Gospel of John mutually influenced each other? How similar and at the same time how different these testimonies are becomes even more evident if their clearest parallel is included in the discussion, namely the designation of Jesus as 'the light' (Gos. Thom. 77:1; John 8:12) and the related metaphors of light.

5. "I am the Light ..." – the Origin and Destination of the Creation

No other saying of the Gospel of Thomas focuses as much the figure of Jesus like Gos. Thom 77. The concise text is designed as a statement by which the Jesus of Thomas of Thomas declares his self-understanding.

> *Gos. Thom. 77*
> (1) Jesus says:
>> "I am the light,
>> that is above all.
>> I am the universe.
>> The universe came fourth out of me,
>> and the universe reached me.
> (2)   Split a piece of wood – I'm there.
> (3)   lift up the stone and you will find me there."[62]

The structure of Gos. Thom. 77 is clearly visible. The introductory statement identifies Jesus as 'the light'. The following statements unfold what is meant by this light. The central thesis of this interpretation of the figure of Jesus is distinctive: Jesus is called the manifestation, origin and destination of all existence (cf. Gos. Thom. 77:1b). The disciples of Jesus should realize that they can find Jesus everywhere. Just as the kingdom (of the Father) is present both within and outside of them (Gos. Thom. 3:3) and within the whole world (Gos. Thom. 113:3), Jesus is accessible

---

62   The Coptic translation documents changes in the text as Gos. Thom. 77:2-3 in P.Oxy 1:23-30 is connected to Gos. Thom. 30. This illustrates the gradual growth of the sayings of the Gospel of Thomas. Cf. I. Miroshnikov, Thomas, 62-70; W. Eisele, Thomas, 165-171; E. E. Popkes, Licht, passim.

everywhere as the omnipresent light[63]. These features of the Gospel of Thomas make it clear that Jesus is not simply seen as an itinerant preacher or a teacher of wisdom in this work. Rather he is described by attributes, which identify him as a divine figure[64]. Accordingly, many debates occurred regarding the question to what extent Gos. Thom. 77 conveys pantheistic ideas[65].

Gos. Thom. 77 indicates how near and at the same time far away this image of Jesus is from the Christology of the Gospel of John. Both Gospels present the statement 'I am the light' (cf. John 8:12). In both Gospels Jesus calls himself the 'Son of the Father' (Gos. Thom. 37:3, 61:3; John 5:19-30; 10:30; 14:8-9; 17:1-5 etc.). But the central message of the Johannine Jesus is that his disciples should believe in him. The believers will be freed from the darkness and will share eternal life (John 1:4-5.9-10; 3:16-18; 8:12 etc.). Instead, the Jesus of the Gospel of Thomas encourages his disciples to realize that they already are 'children of the Father' (Gos. Thom. 3:4-5) and that they become manifestations of that divine light (Gos. Thom. 24:3) [66].

Against the background of the theme of becoming one with Jesus (Gos. Thom. 108), it can also be explained why the depicted features of the Gospel of Thomas embody a Christian interpretation

---

63 The emphasis on the omnipresence of Jesus may also be a reason why Gos. Thom. 77:1 and Gos. Thom. 77:2-3 were connected with each other in the Coptic translation. U.-K. Plisch, Thomasevangelium, 196 summarizes aptly: "Holz spalten und Steine aufheben begegnen dann nicht zufällig im Munde des ‚Zimmermanns' Jesus von Nazareth. Ihr Sinn wäre demnach, dass man Jesus im Alltag der Welt begegnet, eben bei der Arbeit, und zu ihm nicht durch besondere religiöse Übungen oder spirituelle Anstrengungen und Leistungen findet."

64 Cf. S. Gathercole, Nag Hammadi Gospels, 210 regarding Gos. Thom. 61/77: "The picture of Jesus in *Thomas* then, makes it difficult to sustain the 'low christology' view, or the 'no christology' view, because Jesus is thematised, and thematised in remarkable terms, not just as a sage."

65 Regarding the history of these discussions cf. I. Miroshnikov, Thomas, 62-70; 269-273.

66 Regarding the relationship between the metaphors of light within the Gospel of Thomas and the Gospel of John I refer to my preparatory studies in E. E. Popkes, Lichtmetaphorik, passim.

of the Platonic motif of 'becoming like God' (cf. Plato, Theaet. 176 b 1-3 as a point of reference to the motif of ὁμοίωσις θεῷ). In the sense of the anthropology and the metaphors of light within the Gospel of Thomas, all human beings bear the light that showed itself in Jesus. And when they unfold this *lumen internum*, they in turn contribute to the enlightenment of the world. This idea will be explained in the following chapter.

6. "... and it enlightens the whole world."
– the Divine Light within human beings

In the introduction it has been explained to what extent the arrangement of the sayings of the Gospel of Thomas reveals hidden mosaics (cf. 2.10). This can also be demonstrated in regard to the interpretation of Gos. Thom. 24 and Gos. Thom. 77. These sayings are in many ways similiar in content. Strictly speaking, Gos. Thom. 77 can be interpreted as an immediate continuation of Gos. Thom. 24:

> Gos. Thom. 24
> (1) His disciples said to him:
> > "Show us the place where you are
> > for it is necessary for us to seek it."
> (2) He said to them:
> > "Whoever has ears to hear sould hear!
> (3)   There is light within a person of light
> > and it enlightens the whole world.
> > If it does not shine, there is darkness."[67]

Gos. Thom. 24:1 is initiated by a question directly related to the topic of 'seeking and finding' that was already emphasized in the first words of the Gospel of Thomas. The disciples want to be informed about the place where they can find Jesus. The answer can already be seen in the present form and arrangement of Gos. Thom. 24. It becomes even clearer when Gos. Thom. 24 is interpreted against the background of Gos. Thom. 77: that 'place' is the light hidden within them – so *they* are themselves this 'place'. This facet of the Gospel of Thomas is thus a variation of those

---

67   From a grammatical point of view, Gos. Thom. 24:3b can be related to 'light' and 'a person of light' (compare U.-K. Plisch, Thomasevangelium, 196). In connection with the previously explained metaphors of light within Gos. Thom. 50:1; 61:5; 77:1, it is more plausible to choose 'light' as point of reference.

appeals that the disciples of Jesus should recognize themselves. The meaning of the introductory question is emphasized by a formula that also appears in other contexts of the Gospel of Thomas (cf. Gos. Thom. 24:2 with Gos. Thom. 8; 21; 63; 65; 96). The following answer speaks of a light that is hidden in 'human beings of light'. This motif opens up space for different interpretations. It is not explained clearly whether that statement about an 'inner light' is formulated as a general statement about all human beings, or whether it takes only a certain group of people into focus. In this context, too, it becomes clear again that the message of sayings in the Gospel of Thomas depends on which reference texts are chosen as a benchmark of interpretation. So there are e.g. concepts of anthropology according to which the behavior and the cognitive ability of human beings are predestined or determined. In the context of biblical traditions, reference can be made in this regard to features of Paul's anthropology. Paul can appeal to his addressees as 'children of the light' in the sense of his Jewish-Pharisaic background of education and admonish them for a corresponding life-style (1 Thess. 5:5). At the same time, however, he can emphasize that they cannot freely determine their behavior (see, inter alia, Phil 2:12b-13: "... work out your own salvation with fear and trembling. For it is God who causes in you both to will and to work of his good pleasure"[68]).

---

68 Paul most clearly emphasizes his ideas of predestination in Rom 9:6-24; 11:7-10.25-27.32 (especially Rom 9:18: "So then he has mercy on whomever he wills, and he hardens whomever he wills".). Even if it is controversial to what extent these statements merely take on special functions in the reflection of the situation of Israel, which Paul unfolds in the context of Rom 9-11, it is undisputed that these statements became the foundation of various concepts of a doctrine of predestination (on the outline and on contrary interpretations of the motifs of predestination within Paul's theology cf. U. Schnelle, Paulus, 431ff; G. Röhser, Prädestination, 113-176; T. Eskola, Theodicy, passim; for their receptions in the history of dogmatics see e.g. J. Couenhoven, Presdestination, passim; C. Link, Art. Erwählung III. Dogmatisch, 1482-1489; W. Trillhaas, Dogmatik, 235ff; W. Zeindler, Erwählung, 27-96).

However, such ideas are even clearer in the group of texts in which there are many parallels to the Gospel of Thomas, namely in the Johannine writings. The author of the first letter of John distinguishes between 'children of God' and 'children of the devil', which are determined by their nature and behavior (compare 1 John 3:7-10, especially 1 John 3:9: "No one born of God makes a practice of sinning, for God's seed abides in him, and he cannot sin, because he has been born of God"[69]). This dualism corresponds to a motif which occurs within the Fourth Gospel. The Johannine Jesus confronts his Jewish interlocutors, who do not want to believe in him, with a severe accusation (cf. John 8:42-47, especially John 8:44a: "You are of your father the devil, and your will is to do your father's desires"). They can not hear and understand his message because they are not capable of doing so[70]. The idea that human beings are capable of salvation in different ways is also postulated in many extra-canonical testimonies of early Christianity (significant examples for such ideas are the "Valentinian Theories on Classes of Humankind"[71] which differ between so-called 'spiritual persons', 'animate persons', and 'material persons').

Against the background of such ideas of predestination and determination, Gos. Thom. 24:3 would apply to a limited number of people. However, there are two indications that contradict such an interpretation of Gos. Thom. 24. It is already evident in Gos. Thom. 24:3b that the light should benefit the cosmos: that *lumen internum* should enlighten the world. Such a positive statement contradicts a Gnostic interpretation, in which the existing world

---

69 Regarding these features of the Johannine writings cf. U. U. Kaiser, Wiedergeburt, 151-160; 276-284; E. E. Popkes, Liebe, 23-36; 114-120.

70 The literarily stylized conversations of the Johannine Jesus and his interlocutors reflect processes of separations which have shaped the development of the Johannine communities (cf. J. Zumstein, Johannesevangelium, 92f.; F. Mußner, Traktat, 281-292).

71 Cf. I. Dunderberg, Classes of Humankind, 79-92. Furthermore C. Markschies, Valentinus, 146f.; E. Thomassen, Seed, 112f.

is understood as a principally bad creation of a bad creator. According to a Gnostic understanding, those 'particles of light' are supposed to liberate themselves from the kosmos – they should not enlighten the kosmos[72].

However, the positive understanding of the world in Gos. Thom. 24:3 becomes even clearer when the metaphors of light within Gos. Thom. 24 are interpreted against the background of Gos. Thom. 77. If Jesus is understood as a manifestation of the omnipresent light that is the origin of all existence and into which all existence returns, then every human being is also a bearer of that 'inner light'. Otherwise this light would not be omnipresent. The aspects just outlined reveal even clearer the ultimate concept of the 'oneness with Jesus': According to the Gospel of Thomas, the central message of Jesus is that every human being should become a 'light person' who enlightens the world. Although the Gospel of Thomas records a series of sayings that reveal an exceedingly critical attitude towards the world and a bodily existence (see the preceding remarks on Gos. Thom. 56; 80; 87; 112), it does not represent any fundamental condemnation of the created world. Here, too, it corresponds to a Platonic worldview and contradicts a Gnostic criticism of this world and its creator. And here, too, the Gospel of Thomas is close to the Gospel of John, which also reveals a dialectical relationship with the cosmos.

> _Guiding assumption 2.13:_ The Gospel of Thomas understands _all_ human beings as bearers of the divine light that enlightens the world when human beings become like Jesus.

---

72 For this reason, in contrast to my earlier studies, I emphasize that these traits of Gos. Thom. 24; 77 imply positive attitudes to the cosmos that differ fundamentally from Gnostic rejections of the world and its creator (cf. E. E. Popkes, Menschenbild, passim).

However, the metaphors of light within Gos. Thom. 24:3; 77 have to be broadened by another facet, which also reveals the Platonic background of the Gospel of Thomas. According to Gos. Thom. 50:1, human beings are not only bearers of a divine light, but they also come from the divine light. In this respect, the Jesus of the Gospel of Thomas is thus also stylized as the teacher of a Platonic theory of the preexistence and transmigration of souls. This aspect will be explained in the following chapter.

7. "We have come from the Light ..."
– Jesus teaches the Transmigration of Souls

Those sayings in the Gospel of Thomas, which presuppose the notions of a preexistence and transmigration of the immortal souls can impressively demonstrate the platonic interpretation of the figure and message of Jesus. The importance of these motifs is shown not least by the fact that they are discussed in three groups of sayings, which are directly related to each other (Gos. Thom. 18/19; 49/59 and 83/84). Against this background, other sayings can be interpreted which when interpreted separately, seem to be incomprehensible.

A first glimpse of the motif of a preexistence of souls occurs in Gos. Thom. 4:1. However, only initial hints of this idea can be perceived here. The statement that an old person should ask a newborn baby about the place of life remains paradoxical at first sight (cf. the remarks in chapter 3). A different picture emerges when Gos. Thom. 4 is related to those sayings which focus on the understanding of soul, creation and death.

In the order of the sayings chosen for the Coptic translation of the Gospel of Thomas, the connected sayings Gos. Thom. 18; 19 offer the first words of Jesus, in which the idea of a pre-existence of the soul before a physical birth is clearly visible.

Gos. Thom. 18
(1) The disciples say to Jesus:
   "Tell us how our end will be!"
(2) Jesus says:
   "Have you already discovered the beginning,
   that you are now looking for the end?
   For where the beginning is,
   there will be the end too.

(3)   Blessed is he who will stand at the beginning.
      And he will come to know the end
      and will not taste death."

Gos. Thom. 19
(1) Jesus says:
      "Blessed is the one who existed
      before he came into being".
(2)   If you become my disciples (and) listen my words,
      these stones will serve you.
(3)   For there are five trees for you in paradise,
      which do not alter in summer or in winter
      and their leaves do not fall.
(4)   Whoever will recognize them
      will not taste death."

The immediately consecutive sayings, which are closely linked in terms of terminology and content, are initiated by a question of the disciples. They want to know which end or which completion their existence will find. As in Gos. Thom. 51; 113 Jesus' followers ask a question that corresponds to traditional expectations. And just as in those sayings, Jesus' response documents that such an expectation is wrong in principle. Instead the disciples of Jesus should realize the origin of their existence. The knowledge of their beginning will reveal their end and their completion.
The following saying Gos. Thom. 19 focusses a special detail that the disciples of Jesus should recognize in relation to the origin of their existence. Initially Gos. Thom. 19:1 describes one more time the notions of a pre-existence. Afterwards, a motif is mentioned which, at first sight, reminds of the biblical narratives of creation and paradise. However, the motif of five trees, which are not subject to the seasonal cycle of becoming and decaying, has its analogy not directly in Gen 2-3, but in Hellenistic-Jewish and

Gnostic-Manichean interpretations of these traditions[73]. Just as in Gos. Thom. 18:3, Gos. Thom. 19:4 ends in a thesis that incorporates and modifies the promise with which the readers were already confronted in the first words of the Gospel of Thomas: whoever recognizes the origin of his own existence will not suffer the fate of death.

However, the motifs of a preexistence and transmigration of souls are most evident in Gos. Thom. 49; 50. Both sayings have a high relevance for the interpretation of the Gospel of Thomas, which is put up for discussion with this book.

Gos. Thom. 49
(1) Jesus says:
    "Blessed are 'the ones who become oneness'
    the chosen ones,
    for you will find the kingdom.
(2)   Because you come from there,
    and you will return there."

Gos. Thom. 50
(1) Jesus says:
    "If they say to you:
        'Where do you come from?',
    say to them:
        'We have come from the light,
        the place where the light came into being by itself,
        established itself.

---

73 For an overview of possible comparative texts see S. Gathercole, Thomas, 289-296; E. E. Popkes, Menschenbild, 257-342.

and appeared in their image.'[74]

(2)   If they say to you:

'Is it you?',

say:

'We are his children and we are

the chosen ones of the living father.'

(3)   If they ask you:

'What is the sign of your father within you?',

say to them:

'It is movement and repose.'"

Both sayings have central intentions in common. Differences exist on the one hand in the images and concepts used, on the other hand in the thematic culminations. For both texts, the motif
of pre-existence is of fundamental importance. The place of that
preexistence is first referred to by the term 'kingdom' (Gos. Thom.
49:1), which is closely related to the term 'kingdom of God', the
term which was central to early traditions regarding the message
of Jesus. On the other hand, in Gos. Thom. 50:1 the actual home
of Jesus' disciples is called 'the light'[75]. The extraordinary quality
of this light is emphasized by describing it as a divine being: it
emerged out of itself. But this light is not only a purely other-
worldly dimension. It is also present in this world: the light has
manifested itself in 'their images' (cf. Gos. Thom. 50:1b). This
detail already suggests a relationship between the distinction of

---

74 In relation to the final formulation of Gos. Thom. 50:1, C. Tornau, Kritik,
358-359 introduces an alternative interpretation into the discussion, which
postulates a grammatical error at the level of the Coptic translation. He assumes
that the Greek text version worked with an indirectly reflective formulation.
Accordingly, the final formulation could have originally been "and appeared in
our picture". This would be a clear analogy to Gos. Thom. 84.

75 Regarding the Platonic backgrounds of the motifs of 'movement' and 'repose' in Gos. Thom. 50:3, S. J. Patterson, Way, 130 states: "Here is the Platonic
idea of the soul's journey from heaven and its eventual return home. As the
spirit is released from the body, it rises upward. (...) If one can achieve such
harmony, the soul is said to be both moving and at repose (Timaeus 90)."

'archetypes' and 'images' of human existence described in Gos. Thom. 83; 84. Both aspects, in turn, reveal clear analogies with Platonic concepts. Thus, e.g. the 'home-in-the-light' mentioned in Gos. Thom. 50:1 can be described as that 'true light' which, according to Plato, cannot be perceived in this world (see, inter alia, Plato, Phaedo 109 e) [76]. The motif that this light should have manifested itself in the 'images of human beings' corresponds to further central ideas of the Gospel of Thomas. On the one hand, it is close to the motif that human beings carry a *lumen internum* within themselves, which can enlighten the world (cf. the explanation regarding Gos. Thom. 24:3). On the other hand, Gos. Thom. 50:1 corresponds to the motif that Jesus is that omnipresent light from which the creation originates and for which the creation strives back (Gos. Thom. 77:1)[77]. In this regard, 'light' in addition to 'father' is thus a synonym for God.

Guiding assumption 2.14: The Gospel of Thomas interprets the figure of Jesus as *one* incarnation of the 'true light' that, according to Plato, can only be experienced outside this world.

Even more clearly than the aforementioned sayings, Gos. Thom.

---

76 In the myth of a postmortal existence of Plato's dialogue *Phaedo*, Socrates explains this motif immediately before his execution. It can clearly be seen that Plato constructs a reference to the parable of the cave, according to which the 'true light' can only be recognized outside the cave with which he compares the existence in this world. W. Eisele, Jenseitsmythen, 320, states that between these texts innuendos are unmistakable. For more details see E. E. Popkes, Erfahrungen I, 115-118.

77 Regarding the backgrounds of this motif, a peculiar phenomenon can be observed. In relation to the Johannine metaphor of light, it has been debated many times whether there is a connection with the motif of 'true light' in Plato, Phaed. 109 e, especially John 1:9 ἦν τὸ φῶς τὸ ἀληθινόν, ὃ φωτίζει πάντα ἄνθρωπον, ἐρχόμενον εἰς τὸν κόσμον (so already C. H. Dodd, Interpretation, 140; last among others G. H. Van Kooten, Light, 149-194; idem., Anthropology, 56; H. W. Attridge, Platonic Reflections, 277-295). The importance of the relationship between the light metaphors of the Gospel of John and the Gospel of Thomas is hardly questioned (this applies even to the otherwise very good study of the Platonic backgrounds of this work by I. Miroshnikov, Plato, passim).

49 and Gos. Thom. 50 are based on the idea of a transmigration of souls. In the ancient Mediterranean environment and in extra-canonical testimonies of early Christianity, there are various comparative concepts for such an anthropology, especially in those traditions which are close to Platonic and Gnostic beliefs. Likewise, various authors document that in the history of early Christianity such ideas were discussed (see especially Irenaeus of Lyon, Tertullian, Clement of Alexandria, Origen, etc.) [78]. Many of the testimonies found in the Nag Hammadi codices are also based on ideas of a transmigration of souls.

A peculiarity of Gos. Thom. 49, however, is the term *monachos* (ⲘⲞⲚⲀⲬⲞⲤ), which refers to the people who come from that pre-existence and return to that state. The use of *monachos* in Gos. Thom. 16; 49; 75 is already remarkable because it is probably the earliest evidence of this term[79]. In the history of early monasticism which began much later, *monachos* actually referred to a 'monk'. Nevertheless, it would be inappropriate to translate this term in the context of the Gospel of Thomas as 'monk'. Also, the term 'solitary' used in many translations and comments are inaccurate. Such a translation is not fundamentally wrong, but it falls short. Derived from the term μόνας ('monad' or 'unity'), *monachos* should rather be interpreted as a paraphrase of 'becoming one'. The term thus expresses the overcoming of the opposites that characterize the presence of human beings (that is, for example, the overcoming of gender differences, etc.) [80].

---

78 Cf. H. Zander, Seelenwanderung, 126-133; E. E. Popkes, Erfahrungen II, passim.

79 It is hardly surprising that the term *monachos* has always attracted special attention since the discovery of the Coptic Gospel of Thomas. On the history of research and the spectrum of contrary interpretations see S. Gathercole, Thomas, 278-282; E. E. Popkes, Menschenbild, 147-211; I. Miroshinkov, Plato, 116-128.

80 In this respect the term is close to other sayings by Jesus in the Gospel of Thomas, which are hardly understandable on their own (cf. Gos. Thom. 22; 114 etc.).

The motif of overcoming these opposites in the Gospel of Thomas is illustrated by the third saying in which the term *monachos* appears:

Gos. Thom. 75
Jesus says:
>"Many are standing at the door,
>but 'who became oneness'
>will enter the bridal chamber."

Gos. Thom. 75 uses the motif of a married couple entering the bridal chamber. By this, gender differences and how to overcome them are put into focus. In various cultures of the ancient Mediterranean environment of the Gospel of Thomas, this motif is seen as the symbol of the union of man and woman, from which new life emerges[81].

At first glance, Gos. Thom. 75 seems like a parallel to the parable of the wise and unwise brides or bridesmaids, narrated in Matt 25:1-13. However, the motif is also known from Gnostic traditions, especially in Valentianism, where the bridal chamber is understood as one of five sacraments[82]. The picture of the bridal room describes the transition from the entry into the 'repose' and thus into the final consummation of human existence. Remarkably enough, this motif is developed in the Gospel of Philipp which directly follows the Gospel of Thomas in the second codex of the Nag Hammadi writings (Gos. Phil. 61; 66-68; 73; 76; 79; 80; 82; 87; 95; 102; 122; 124; 127). This can be seen as further indication that the Coptic translation of the Gospel of Thomas handed down in the second codex of the Nag Hammadi writings experienced revisions that produced a thematic entanglement of the individual treatises. Or to paraphrase this aspect in regard to

---

81 Cf. R. Zimmermann, Geschlechtermetaphorik, passim.
82 Cf. E. Thomassen, Seed, 348-353.

the metaphor that was explained in chapter 2.7: Gos. Thom. 75 is one of those sayings of the Gospel of Thomas in which 'Jesus on his way to Gnosticism' is already far advanced. But the fact that this path began with Plato, however, is clearly illustrated by the unit of sayings Gos. Thom. 83; 84.

Gos. Thom. 83
(1) Jesus says:
> "The images are visible to human beings;
> but the light that is in them is hidden by the image[83].
(2) The light of the father will reveal itself
> but his image is hidden by his light."

Gos. Thom. 84
(1) Jesus says:
> "When you see your likeness,
> you are full of joy.
(2) But when you see your images
> that came into being before you
> – they neither die, nor do they appear –
> how much will you bear?"

Gos. Thom. 83; 84 is the third complex of sayings, which deals with the themes of a preexistence and transmigration of souls: The corporeal and mortal dimensions of existence correspond to 'images' (Gos. Thom. 83:1a;84:1), whereas the immortal 'archetypes' correspond to the animated and immortal dimension of existence (cf. Gos. Thom. 84:2). However, both sayings are again examples of the fact that the Gospel of Thomas can be interpreted in different ways. The meaning of a saying is influenced by the framework of interpretation. If one refers to Gnostic interpreta-

---

83 Regarding the form of the text, the structure and the translation of the transition from Gos. Thom. 83:1 to Gos. Thom. 83:2 see most recently I. Miroshnikov, Thomas, 222ff.; E. E. Popkes, Menschenbild, 228-231.

tions of the biblical creation narratives Gen 1-3, Gos. Thom. 83; 84 can be interpreted as an expression of a Gnostic anthropology. With regard to the composition of the second codex of the Nag Hammadi writings, such a Gnostic reformulation of the biblical narratives of creation is formulated in the long version of the Apocryphon of John (NHC II, 1) which is put just before the Coptic translation of the Gospel of Thomas. This can be taken as an indication of how those persons responsible for putting together the second Nag Hammadi Codex interpreted Gos. Thom. 83; 84. It does not mean, however, that both sayings necessarily have to be interpreted this way[84].

If e.g. Gos. Thom. 83; 84 are interpreted directly against the background of Platonic traditions, they can be interpreted as a variation of the motif that in this world, all forms of existence are to be understood merely as emphemeral images of imperishable archetypes. However, these immortal dimensions represent a complexity that can only be perceived to a limited extent during the existence in this world[85]. With regard to Gos. Thom. 83; 84, it is important to emphasize one detail in particular: The three units of sayings Gos. Thom. 18/19; Gos. Thom. 49/50 and Gos. Thom. 83/84 convey quite comparable ideas with varying metaphors and concepts. In the last part of this triad, however, a new aspect is emphasized. Gos. Thom. 83:2 ends with the statement that the 'light of the Father' will be revealed. If this detail is set against the background of the outlined interpretations of Gos. Thom. 24; 77; 108 and the philosophy of Plato, it is possible to see what

---

84 Concerning the spectrum of possible backgrounds of Gos. Thom. 83/84 and the relation between the Coptic translation of the Gospel of Thomas (NHC II,2) and the immediately before arranged long version of the Apocryphon of John (NHC II,1) I refer to my preliminary work in E. E. Popkes, Menschenbild, 227-332.

85 C. W. Hedrick, Thomas, 148 recognizes not only an analogy to Plato's parable of the cave, but also to the corresponding features of the parable of the sun with which Plato illustrates among other things the idea of the good: "... in the case of Thomas, the Good equals the Father ...".

hope the Gospel of Thomas intends to convey for the existence in this world. As explained earlier, Jesus is interpreted as the earthly presence of that 'true light', which – according to Plato – can be experienced outside this world (Plato, Phaed. 109 e). This light is omnipresent and thus also present in every human being (Gos. Thom. 24:3; 77). When Jesus' disciples become like Jesus (Gos. Thom. 108), they too become 'people of light' and 'revelations of the light of the Father' (Gos. Thom. 84:2). This light will enlighten the world (Gos. Thom. 24:3). Thus, the central message of the Gospel of Thomas is that all human beings can become an earthly presence of that light from which they originally came, to which they return and which Jesus incarnated (Gos. Thom. 28; 49; 50:1; 77)[86].

In this respect, the Gospel of Thomas not only represents a special form of an early Christian tradition to be marginalized as 'Vulgär-Platonismus' ('vulgar Platonism'). Rather, it is also about a new formation of Platonism, in the form of a 'Platonic Christianity'. And according to the Gospel of Thomas, the founder of Platonic Christianity was none other than Jesus himself.

> *Guiding assumption 2.15:* According to the Gospel of Thomas, Jesus is the founder of a 'Platonic Christianity'.

---

86 Such an idea becomes particularly evident when these traits of the Gospel of Thomas are interpreted against the background of Plato's doctrine of the transmigration of souls, which assume a gradual growth of souls (in detail E. E. Popkes, Erfahrungen I, 118-131; idem, Platonisches Christentum, passim). According to I. Miroshnikov, Plato, 256f. the arrangement of the texts Gos. Thom. 50:1 - Gos. Thom. 22:6 - Gos. Thom. 83:1; 84:2 - Gos. Thom. 83:2 mirrors an eschatological expectation: "Thomasine protology and eschatology do not duplicate each other; the Gospel of Thomas does not envision salvation as merely returning to the original state. Rather, there is an antithetic parallelism between protology and eschatology; the end is, in a way, the opposite of the beginning."

8. Summary and outlooks

The central features of the Platonic interpretation of the figure and the message of Jesus, which are present in the Gospel of Thomas will be summarized in three steps. First, the Platonic features of the Gospel of Thomas are summarized (8.1) and illustrated visualy (8.2). Finally, the guiding theses formulated in the course of the interpretation are recapitulated (8.3).

8.1 The Platonic Interpretation of the figure and message of Jesus in the Gospel of Thomas

The Gospel of Thomas conveys a Platonic interpretation of the figure and message of Jesus. Its central theses can be explained based on his metaphors of light. According to the Gospel of Thomas, Jesus is the omnipresent light and the All – the entire creation has emerged from him and strives back to him (Gos. Thom. 77:1). Jesus is interpreted as an earthly presence of that 'true light' which, according to Plato's theology and anthropology, can only be experienced outside the present world (Plato, Phaed. 109 e). The Jesus of the Gospel of Thomas, however, emphasizes that this light is hidden in all human beings (Gos. Thom. 24:3). They come from that light and go back there (Gos. Thom. 49; 50:1). For their part, they should contribute to the enlightenment of the existing world (Gos. Thom. 24:3; 83; 84).

The mentioned facets of the Gospel of Thomas are based on the motif of 'becoming like Jesus' (Gos. Thom. 108:1f; 13:4-8; 61:3-5). Whoever becomes like Jesus will get access to a universal knowledge and becomes himself a 'human being of light' and 'revelation of the divine light' (Gos. Thom. 24:3; 61:5; 108:3). An obstacle to this development can be the cosmic and physical dimension of human existence (Gos. Thom. 7; 56; 80; 87; 112). Because of this, human beings have to distinguish between their mortal images and their immortal archetypes (Gos. Thom. 83; 84). By becoming one with Jesus, they unfold the light that is hidden inside of them and that can enlighten the world (Gos. Thom. 24:3; 61:5). The Gospel of Thomas also conveys the oldest testimonies of the term *monachos* (**MONⲀXOC**) which was of great importance within this history of early Christian monasticism. Nevertheless, this term should not be translated as 'monk'. Within the Gospel of Thomas, *monachos* first expresses that the true disciples of Jesus are exposed to loneliness and isolation (compare the resemblance of the use of *monachos* in Gos. Thom. 16:4; 49:1; 75 with Gos. Thom. 8; 23; 30; 107; etc.). This aspect corresponds to the phenomenon that in the Gospel of Thomas, larger communities and hierarchies are critically evaluated (Gos. Thom. 3; 13). However, the term *monachos* also has a second level that conveys the understanding of salvation and perfection upon which the Gospel of Thomas is based. The *monachos*-statements are thematically related to those sayings of Jesus that speak of an overcoming of the individual characteristics of human existence, in particular the overcoming of the gender differences between man and woman (see the correspondence of the *monachos*-statements in Gos. Thom. 16:4; 49:1; 75 with Gos. Thom. 4; 11:4; 22:4-7; 48; 106; 114). By returning to the divine unity from which they originate (cf., inter alia, Gos. Thom. 49; 50:1f.) people overcome individuality. In view of this, the term *monachos* can be understood as a *terminus technicus* for the image of human beings in the Gospel of Thomas, with which the perfected disciples of Jesus are designated. They thus return to the divine unity (μόνας) from which they originate (Gos. Thom. 49). This perfection of human existence is referred to as the motif of the bridal chamber, which describes the abolition of gender difference (cf. Gos. Thom. 75).

In this sense, a saying of the Gospel of Thomas, which at first glance is difficult to understand, can be interpreted relatively easily, namely Gos. Thom. 42. This by far shortest saying of Jesus in the Gospel of Thomas simply confronts his readers with the demand to become 'passing by'. Against the background of the biblical Gospels, such a demand may seem puzzling. The situation is different, however, if one interprets the same against the background of the formula '... from here to there ... ' (ἐνθένδε ἐκεῖσε), which expresses the 'core of all Platonism'.[87].

However, the Platonic interpretation of the figure and message of Jesus also suggests why many of the concepts that are central to the biblical Gospels cannot have any meaning for the Gospel of Thomas (especially the interpretation of the death of Jesus as an atonement and the idea of a bodily resurrection). In particular, the Gospel of Thomas and the Gospel of John appear as contrasting parallels, whose authors have mutually influenced each other in their development (especially regarding the contrary concepts of incarnation, of becoming like Jesus or God and of the understanding of faith and self-knowledge). They impressively demonstrate how canonical and extra-canonical testimonies of early Christianity reflect 'hidden discourses', whose revival can give valuable impulses to theology and church. This aspect will be explained in the fourth sub-volume of the series 'Platonic Christianity'.

---

87 Regarding this motif cf. footnote 54. S. J. Patterson, Way, 131 states: "This is not Gnosticism; it is simply a Jewish take on Platonism."

8.2 Schematic diagram of the Platonic Interpretation of the figure and message of Jesus in the Gospel of Thomas

All existence comes out of the divine light
and strives back there.
(Gos. Thom. 50:1; 77:1)

↓

All human beings carry the divine light in themselves.
(Gos. Thom. 24:3)

↓

Jesus is *one* incarnation of the divine light.
(Gos. Thom. 77)

↓

When human beings understand the secret message of Jesus
and realize themselves, they become like Jesus and
the hidden knowledge will be revealed to them.
(Gos. Thom. 108, corresponding to Gos. Thom. 3; 5; 92 etc.).

↓

Human beings have to distinguish between
their mortal-physical images and their immortal-psychic archetypes.
(Gos. Thom. 84).

↓

Human beings must not be dominated by the physical
and cosmic dimensions of their existence in this world.
(Gos. Thom. 7; 56; 80; 87; 112 etc.)

↓

The divine light will continue to reveal itself.
(Gos. Thom. 83)

↓

The light hidden in human beings can enlighten the world.
(Gos. Thom. 24:3)

8.3 Summary of the guiding assumptions

In the summaries of the sub-volumes of the series 'Platonic Christianity', the guiding assumption, which connects all contributions, is recapitulated first. The count of the following guiding assumptions is based on the ordinal numbers of the individual volumes.

> Guiding assumption of all volumes of the series 'Platonic Christianity': Scientific discourses regarding the phenomenon of 'death' in general and regarding so-called 'near-death experiences' in particular open up approaches to new kinds of Platonic-Christian religiosity.

Guiding assumption 2.1: The Gospel of Thomas is one of the oldest testimonies of a Platonic Christianity whose message should be reconsidered today.

Guiding assumption 2.2: The author of the Gospel of John stylizes Thomas as a symbol of a doubter to criticize a contrary interpretation of the figure and message of Jesus.

Guiding assumption 2.3: The collective term 'Thomas-Christianity' describes different religious communities, which refer to the Apostle Thomas and who are not represented by the writings of the New Testament.

Guiding assumption 2.4: Even if its surviving text witnesses and traditions are relatively young and show gradual growth, the Gospel of Thomas represents positions within early Christian discourses that occur indirectly already in canonical testimonies.

Guiding assumption 2.5: Apocryphal testimonies such as the Gospel of Thomas reveal early Christian discourses that should be revived today.

Guiding assumption 2.6: Even if the biblical Gospels do not convey uniform images of Jesus, they are fundamentally different from the image of Jesus in the Gospel of Thomas.

Guiding assumption 2.7: For the Gospel of Thomas, the historical circumstances of Jesus' life, the faith in Jesus as Christ, the interpretation of the death of Jesus as atonement and the faith in a bodily resurrection of Jesus have no relevance.

Guiding assumption 2.8: The image of Jesus in the Gospel of John can be interpreted as a direct contrast to the image of Jesus in the Gospel of Thomas.

Guiding assumption 2.9: In the Gospel of Thomas, the figure and message of Jesus is interpreted not within the framework of biblical traditions, but within the framework of Platonism.

Guiding assumption 2.10: The Gospel of Thomas embodies a new approach in the history of Platonism and early Christianity that can be named 'Platonic Christianity'.

Guiding assumption 2.11: The developments inspired by the early Jewish itinerant preacher Jesus of Nazareth can only be adequately understood by considering the Gospel of Thomas and the Gospel of John.

Guiding assumption 2.12: The Gospel of Thomas conveys central ideas of Platonism as a message of Jesus, above all the ideas of the immortality of the soul, of becoming like God, of the differentiation between immortale archetypes and mortal images and of the knowledge of the 'true light'.

Guiding assumption 2.13: The Gospel of Thomas understands _all_ human beings as bearers of the divine light that enlightens the world when human beings become like Jesus.

Guiding assumption 2.14: The Gospel of Thomas interprets the figure of Jesus as _one_ incarnation of the 'true light' that, according to Plato, can only be experienced outside this world.

Guiding assumption 2.15: According to the Gospel of Thomas, Jesus is the founder of a 'Platonic Christianity'.

9. Abbreviations

The abbreviations used in this study follow those in *The SBL Handbook of Style for biblical Studies and Related Disciplines; Second Edition* (Atlanta, Georgia: SBL Press. 2014), with following additions:

The abbreviations for book series, journals etc. are based on S. M. Schwertner, Internationales Abkürzungsverzeichnis für Theologie und Grenzgebiete, 2. Aufl., Berlin/New York: Walter de Gruyter, 1992 (although in the citation of biblical books 1 John etc. is always chosen instead of I Joh).

10. Bibliography

10.1 Text editions and translations of the Gospel of Thomas

Attridge, H. W., 'The Gospel According to Thomas. Appendix: The Greek Fragments', in B. Layton (ed.), *Nag Hammadi Codex II,2-7, Bd. 1: Gospel According to Thomas, Gospel according to Philip, Hypostasis of the Archons and Indexes* (NHS XX; The Coptic Gnostic Library; Leiden: Brill, 1989), 93-128.

Bethge, H.-G., 'Evangelium Thomae Copticum', in K. Aland u. a., eds. *Synopsis quattuor Evangeliorum. Locis parallelis evangeliorum apocryporum et patrum adhibitis edidit*, Stuttgart 1996, 517-546.

Layton, B./T. O. Lambdin, 'The Gospel According to Thomas', in B. Layton (ed.), *Nag Hammadi Codex II,2-7, Bd. 1: Gospel According to Thomas, Gospel according to Philip, Hypostasis of the Archons and Indexes* (NHS XX; Leiden: Brill, 1989), 52-93.

Leipoldt, J., *Das Evangelium nach Thomas: koptisch und deutsch* (TU 101; Berlin, Akademie, 1967).

Robinson, J. M., ed. *The Facsimile Edition of the Nag Hammadi Codices: Bd. 2: Kodex II; publ. under the auspices of the department of Antiquites of the Arab Republic of Egypt* (Leiden: Brill, 1974).

Schröter, J., 'Die Oxyrhynchus-Papyri I 1, IV 654 und IV 655 (P.Oxy. I 1; IV 654 und IV 655)', in Schröter, J./C. Markschies, *Antike christliche Apokryphen in deutscher Übersetzung, Band 1: Evangelien und Verwandtes; Teilband 1; 7. Auflage der von Edgar Hennecke begründeten und von Wilhelm Schneemelcher fortgeführten Sammlung der neutestamentlichen Apokryphen* (Tübingen: Siebeck, 2012), 523-526.

Schröter, J./H.-G. Bethge, 'Das Evangelium nach Thomas', in H.-M. Schenke, *Nag Hammadi Deutsch (hrsg. durch die Berlin-Branden-burgische Akademie der Wissenschaften, eingeleitet und übersetzt von Mitgliedern des Berliner Arbeitskreises für Koptisch-Gnostische Schriften; hrsg. von H.-M. Schenke/H.-G. Bethge/U. U. Kaiser (Kop-tische-gnostische Schriften 2: NHC 1,1-5,1; GCS N. F., Bd. 8* (Berlin/ New York: Walter de Gruyter, 2001), 151-181.

Schröter, J.,/H.-G. Bethge, 'Das Evangelium nach Thomas' (Tho-masevangelium [NHC II,2 p. 32,10-51,28]) Oxyrhynchus-Papyri I 1, IV 654 und IV 655 (P.Oxy. I 1; IV 654 und IV 655)', in J. Schrö-ter/C. Markschies, *Antike christliche Apokryphen in deutscher Übersetzung, Band 1: Evangelien und Verwandtes; Teilband 1, 7. Auflage der von Edgar Hennecke begründeten und von Wilhelm Schneemelcher fortgeführten Sammlung der neutestamentlichen Apokryphen* (Tübingen: Mohr Siebeck, 2012), 483-522.

10.2 Secondary literature

Asgeirsson, J. M./A. DeConick/R. Uro, eds. *Thomasine traditions in antiquity. The social and cultural world of the Gospel of Thomas* (NHMS 59; Leiden: Brill, 2006).

Attridge, H. W., '"Seeking" and "asking" in Q, Thomas, and John', in J. M. Asgeirsson/K. de Troyer/M. W. Meyer eds. *From Quest to Q, Festschrift J. M. Robinson* (BEThL 146; Leuven: Peeters 2000), 295-302.

Attridge, H. W., 'The Original Language of the Acts of Thomas', in Idem/J. J. Collins/T. Tobin eds. *Of Scribes and Scrolls. Studies on the Hebrew Bible, Intertestamental Judaism, and Christian Or-igins. Festschrift J. Strugnell* (College Theology Society Resources in Religion 5; Lanham, Maryland: Univ.-Press of America, 1990), 241-250.

Attridge, H. W., 'Stoic and Platonic Reflections on Naming in Early Christianity Circles: Or: What's in a Name?', in T. Engberg-Pedersen eds. *From Stoicism to Platonism* (Cambridge: Cambridge University Press, 2017), 277-295.

Bacht, H., *Das Vermächtnis des Ursprungs, Bd. 1: Studien zum frühen Mönchtum; Bd. 2: Pachomius und sein Werk* (Studien zur Theologie des geistlichen Lebens 5 bzw. 8; Würzburg: Heinrich, 1972 bzw. 1983).

Barns, J. W. B./G. M. Brown/J. C. Shelten eds. *Nag Hammadi Codices: Greek and coptic Papyri from the Cartonage of the Covers* (NHS 16; Brill: Leiden, 1984).

Bauckham, R., 'James and the Jerusalem Community': in O. Skarsaune/R. Hvalvik eds. *Jewish Believers in Jesus* (Peabody, Mass.: Hendrickson Publishers, 2007), 55-95.

Bauckham, R., *The Testimony of the Beloved Disciple: Narrative, History, and Theology in the Gospel of John* (Grand Rapids, Mi.: Baker Academics, 2007).

Bonnes, W., *Caused to believe: the Doubting Thomas story as the climax of John's Christological narrative* (Biblical Interpretation Series 62; Leiden: Brill, 2002).

Bremmer, J. N. eds. *The apocryphal Acts of Thomas* (Studies on early christian apocrypha 6; Leuven: Peeters, 2001).

Brown, R. E., 'The Gospel of Thomas and St. John's Gospel', in *NTS* 9 (1962/63), 155-177.

Carlson, S. C., 'Origen's Use of the Gospel of Thomas', in J. H. Charlesworth/L. M. McDonald eds. *Sacra Scriptura: How 'Non-Canonical' Texts Functioned in Early Judaism and Early Christianity* (Jewish and Christian Textes 20; London: Bloomsbury, 2014), 137-151.

Charlesworth, J. H., *The Beloved Disciple: Whose Witness Validates the Gospel of John?* (Valley Forge, Pa.: Trinity Press International, 1995).

Chilton, B., 'The gospel according to Thomas as a source of Jesus' teaching', in D. Wenham, ed. *The Jesus tradition outside the gospels* (Gospel perspectives 5; Sheffield: JSOT Press, 1985), 155-175.

Chilton, B./C. A. Evans eds. *Studying the Historical Jesus. Evaluations of the state of current research* (NTTS 19; Leiden/New York/ Köln: Brill, 1994).

Davies, S. L., *The Gospel of Thomas and Christian Wisdom* (New York: Seabury Press, 1983).

DeConick, A. D., *Voices of the Mystics. Early Christian Discourse in the Gospel of John and Thomas and other Ancient Christian Literature* (JSNT.S 157; Sheffield: Sheffield Acad. Press, 2001).

DeConick, A. D., 'On the brink of the apocalypse: A preliminary examination of the earliest speeches in the Gospel of Thomas', in J. A. Asgeirsson/A. D. De Conick/R. Uro eds. *Thomasine traditions in antiquity. The social and cultural world of the Gospel of Thomas* (NHMS 59; Leiden: Brill, 2006), 93-118.

DeConick, A. D., '"Blessed are those who have not seen" (Jn 20:29): Johannine dramatization of an early Christian discourse', in J. D. Turner/A. McGuire eds. *The Nag Hammadi library after fifty years. Proceedings of the 1995 Society of Biblical Literature commemoration* (NHS 44; Leiden/New York/Köln: Brill, 1997), 381-398.

DeConick, A. D., 'The yoke saying in the gospel of Thomas 90', in *VigChr* 44 (1990), 280-294.

DeConick, A. D., *Seek to see him. Ascent and Vision Mysticism in the gospel of Thomas* (SVigChr 33; Leiden: Brill, 1996).

DeConick, A. D., 'The original Gospel of Thomas', in *VigChr* 56 (2002), 167-199.

DeConick, A. D., 'John rivals Thomas. From community conflict to gospel narrative', in R. T. Fortna/T. Thatcher eds. *Jesus in Johannine tradition* (Louisville: Westminster, 2001), 303-311.

DeConick, A. D., *The Original Gospel of Thomas in Translation. With a commentary and New English Translation of the Complete Gospel* (LNTS 287; London: T & T Clark, New York, 2006).

Couenhoven, J., *Predestination: Guide for the Perplexed* (London: T & T Clark Bloomsbury Publishing, 2018).

Dodd, C. H., *The Interpretation of the Fourth Gospel* (Cambrigde: Cambridge Univ. Press., 1953).

Dörrie, H., *Die geschichtlichen Wurzeln des Platonismus* (Band 1), in Idem/M. Baltes eds. *Der Platonismus in der Antike*, Bände 1-6 (Stuttgart/Bad Cannstatt: Frommann-Holzboog, 1987).

Drijvers, H. J. W., 'Die Thomasakten', in W. Schneemelcher, ed. *Neutestamentliche Apokryphen in deutscher Übersetzung, Bd. II: Apostolisches, Apokalypsen und Verwandtes* (Tübingen: Mohr Siebeck, 1999), 289-367.

Drijvers, H. J. W., 'Art. Thomas, Apostel', in *TRE 33* (2002), 430-433.

Dunderberg, I., 'Valentinian Theories on Classes of Humankind', in Idem, *Gnostic Morality Revisited* (WUNT 347; Tübingen: Mohr Siebeck, 2015), 79-92.

Dunderberg, I., 'John and Thomas in Conflict?', in J. D. Turner/A. McGuire (ed.), *The Nag Hammadi Library after Fifty Years: Preceedings of the 1995 Society of Biblical Literature Commemoration* (NHMS XLIV; Leiden/New York/Köln: Brill, 1997), 361-380.

Dunderberg, I., 'Thomas' I-sayings and the gospel of John', in R. Uro ed. *Thomas at the crossroads. Essays on the Gospel of Thomas* (Studies of the New Testament and its world; Edinburgh: Clark, 1998), 33-64.

Dunderberg, I., 'From Thomas to Valentinus: Genesis exegesis in Fragment 4 of Valentinus and its relationship to the Gospel of Thomas', in J. A. Asgeirsson/A. D. De Conick/R. Uro eds. *Thomasine traditions in antiquity. The social and cultural world of the Gospel of Thomas* (NHMS 59; Leiden: Brill, 2006), 221-237.

Dunderberg, I., 'Thomas and the Beloved disciple', in R. Uro, ed. *Thomas at the crossroads. Essays on the Gospel of Thomas* (Studies of the New Testament and its world; Edinburgh 1998), 65-88.

Dunderberg, I., *The Beloved Disciple in Conflict? Revisiting the Gospel of John and Thomas* (New York: Oxford Univ. Press, 2006).

Eisele, W., 'Ziehen, Führen und Verführen: eine begriffs- und motivgeschichtliche Untersuchung zu EvThom 3,1', in J. Frey/E. E. Popkes/J. Schröter eds. *Das Thomasevangelium: Entstehung – Rezeption – Theologie* (BZNW 157; Berlin: Walter de Gruyter, 2008), 380-415.

Eisele, W., 'Jenseitsmythen bei Platon und Plutarch', in M. Lang/M. Labahn eds. *Lebendige Hoffnung – ewiger Tod?! Jenseitsvorstellungen im Hellenismus, Judentum und Christentum* (ABG 24; Leipzig: Evang. Verl. Anst., 2007), 315-339.

Eisele, W., *Welcher Thomas? Studien zur Text- und Überlieferungsgeschichte des Thomasevangeliums* (WUNT 259; Tübingen: Mohr Siebeck, 2010).

Eisele, W., ed. *Die Sextussprüche und ihre Verwandten. Eingeleitet, übersetzt und mit interpretierenden Essays versehen von Wilfried Eisele, Yury Arzhanov, Michael Durst und Thomas Pitour* (SAPERE 26; Tübingen: Mohr Siebeck, 2015).

Emmel, S., 'The Coptic Gnostic Texts as Witnesses to the Production and Transmission of Gnostic (and Other) Traditions', in J. Frey/E. E. Popkes/J. Schröter eds. *Das Thomasevangelium: Entstehung – Rezeption – Theologie* (BZNW 157; Berlin: Walter de Gruyter, 2008), 33-49.

Engberg-Pedersen, T., *John and Philosophy: a new Reading of the Fourth Gospel* (Oxford: Oxford Univ. Press, 2017).

Eskola, T., *Theodicy and Predestination in Pauline Soteriology* (WUNT II/100; Tübingen: Mohr Siebeck, 1998).

Fieger, M., *Das Thomasevangelium. Einleitung, Kommentar und Systematik* (NTA 22; Münster: Aschendorff, 1991).

Fröhlich, B., *Selbsterkenntnis und Lebenspraxis: zur apollinischen und platonischen Ethik* (Göttingen: Vandenhoeck & Ruprecht, 2017).

Gärtner, B., *The Theology of the Gospel according to Thomas* (London: Collins, 1961).

Gagné, A., 'The Gospel of Thomas and the New Testament', in J.-M. Roessli/T. Nicklas eds. *Christian Apocrypha: Receptions of the New Testament in Ancient Christian Apocrypha* (Novum Testamentum Patristicum 26; Göttingen: Vandenhoeck & Ruprecht, 2014), 27-40.

Garitte, G., 'Le martyre grégorien de l'apôtre Thomas', in *Muséon* 83 (1970), 497-532.

Gathercole, S., *The Gospel of Thomas: Introduction and Commentary* (TENT 11; Leiden/Boston: Brill, 2014).

Gathercole, S., 'The Nag Hammadi Gospels', in J. Schröter/K. Schwarz eds. *Die Nag-Hammadi-Schriften in der Literatur- und Theologiegeschichte des frühen Christentums* (STAC 106; Tübingen: Mohr Siebeck, 2017), 199-218.

Hartenstein, J., *Charakterisierung im Dialog: Maria Magdalena, Petrus, Thomas und die Mutter Jesu im Johannesevangelium im Kontext anderer frühchristlicher Darstellungen* (NTOA 64; Göttingen: Vandenhoeck & Ruprecht, 2007).

Hedrick, C. W., *Unlocking the Secrets of the Gospel according to Thomas: a radical faith for a New Age* (Eugene, Or., Cascade Books, 2010).

Hedrick, C. W., 'Gnostic Proclivities in the Greek Life of Pachomius and the Sitz im Leben of the Nag Hammadi Library', in *NT 22* (1980), 78-94.

Hengel, M., 'Jakobus der Herrenbruder – der erste „Papst"?', in idem, *Kleine Schriften 3: Paulus und Jakobus* (WUNT 141; Tübingen: Mohr Siebeck, 2002), 549-582.

Hengel, M., *Die johanneische Frage. Ein Lösungsversuch. Mit einem Beitrag zur Apokalypse von J. Frey* (WUNT 67; Tübingen: Mohr Siebeck, 1993).

Holmén, T./S. E. Porter eds. *Handbook for the study of Historical Jesus* (Leiden/Boston: Brill, 2011).

Hurtado, L., 'The Greek Fragments of the Gospel of Thomas as Artefacts: Papyrological Observations on Papyrus Oxyrhynchus 1, Papyrus Oxyrhynchus 654 and Papyrus Oxyrhynchus 655', in J. Frey/E. E. Popkes/J. Schröter eds. *Das Thomasevangelium: Entstehung – Rezeption – Theologie* (BZNW 157; Berlin: Walter de Gruyter, 2008), 19-32.

Jackson, H. M., *The lion becomes man. The Gnostic leontomorphic creator and the Platonic tradition* (SBL.DS 81; Atlanta, Ga.: Scholars Press, 1985).

Kaiser, U. U., *Die Rede von Wiedergeburt im Neuen Testament: ein metapherntheoretisch orientierter Neuansatz nach 100 Jahren Forschungsgeschichte* (WUNT 413; Tübingen: Mohr Siebeck, 2018).

King, K. L., *What is Gnosticism?* (Cambridge, Mass.: Belknap Press of Harvard Univ. Press 2003).

Klauck, H.-J., *Die religiöse Umwelt des Urchristentums I/II* (KSt-

Th 9; Stuttgart/Berlin/New York: Walter de Gruyter, 1995 bzw. 1996).

Klauck, H.-J., *Apokryphe Evangelien: eine Einführung* (Stuttgart: Verl. Kath. Bibelwerk, 2002).

Van Kooten, G. H., "The 'True light which enlightens everyone' (John 1:9): John, Genesis, the Platonic Notion of the True/Noetic Light and the Allegory of the Cave in Plato's Republic", in Idem, ed. *The Creation of Heaven and Earth: Reinterpretations of Genesis I in the Context of Judaism, Ancient Philosophy, Christianity and Modern Physics* (Themes in Biblical Narrative 8; Leiden: Brill, 2005, 149-194).

Van Kooten, G. H., *Paul's Anthropology in context: the image of God, assimilation to God and tripartite man in ancient Judaism, ancient philosophy and early Christianity* (WUNT 232; Tübingen: Mohr Siebeck, 2008).

Kunath, F., *Die Präexistenz Jesu im Johannesevangelium: Struktur und Theologie eines johanneischen Motivs* (BZNW 212; Berlin/Boston: de Gruyter, 2016).

Layton, B., *The Gnostic Scriptures. A New Translation with Annotations and Introductions* (London: SCM Pr., 1987).

Layton, B. ed. *Nag Hammadi Codex II,2-7 together with XIII,2*, Brit. Lib. Or. 4926 (1) and P. Oxy. 1, 654, 655* (NHS 20; Leiden: Brill, etc. 1989).

Layton, B., 'Introduction', in Idem (ed.), *Nag Hammadi Codex II,2-7 together with XIII,2*, Brit. Lib. Or. 4926 (1) and P. Oxy. 1, 654, 655* (NHS 20; Leiden: Brill, etc. 1989).

Link, C., 'Art. Erwählung III. Dogmatisch', in *RGG⁴ 2* (1999), 1482-1489.

Lührmann, D./E. Schlarb, *Fragmente apokryph gewordener Evangelien. In griechischer und lateinischer Sprache; übersetzt und eingeleitet in Zusammenarbeit mit E. Schlarb* (MThS Studien 59; Marburg: Elwert, 2000).

Luijendijk, A., 'Buried and Raised: Gospel of Thomas Logion 5 and Resurrection', in E. Iricinschi/L. Jenott/N. D. Lewis/P. Townsend eds. *Beyond the Gnostic Gospels: Studies Building on the Work of Elaine Pagels* (STAC 82; Tübingen: Mohr Siebeck, 2013), 272-296.

Lundhaug, H./J. Lance, *The Monastic Origins of the Nag Hammadi Codices* (STAC 97; Tübingen: Mohr Siebeck, 2015).

Markschies, C., *Valentinus Gnosticus? Untersuchungen zur valentinianischen Gnosis mit einem Kommentar zu den Fragmenten Valentins* (WUNT 65; Tübingen: Mohr Siebeck, 1992).

Markschies, C., *Die Gnosis* (C. H. Beck-Wissen 2173; München: Beck, 2001).

Markschies, C., 'Offene Fragen zur historischen und literaturgeschichtlichen Einordnung der Nag-Hammadi-Schriften', in J. Schröter/K. Schwarz eds. *Die Nag-Hammadi-Schriften in der Literatur- und Theologiegeschichte des frühen Christentums* (STAC 106; Tübingen: Mohr Siebeck, 2017), 15-36.

Martin, G. M., *Das Thomas-Evangelium: ein spiritueller Kommentar* (Stuttgart: Radius.Verl., 1998).

Mayordomo, M., 'Kluge Mädchen kommen überall hin ... (Von den zehn Jungfrauen) – Mt 25,1-13', in R. Zimmermann ed. *Kompen-*

dium der Gleichnisse Jesu; 2. korrigierte und um Literatur ergänzte Auflage (Gütersloh: Gütersloher Verlagshaus, 2015), 488-503.

Ménard, J.-É., *L'Évangile selon Thomas* (NHS 5; Leiden: Brill, 1975).

Miroshnikov, I., *The Gospel of Thomas and Plato: a study of the impact of Platonism on the 'Fifth Gospel'* (NHMS 93; Leiden/Boston 2018).

Mußner, F., *Traktat über die Juden* (überarbeitete Neuauflage der Erstauflage von 1979; Göttingen: Vandenhoeck & Ruprecht, 2009).

Nicklas, T., 'Beyond Canon. Christian Apocrypha and Pilgrimage', in Idem/C. R. Moss/C. Tuckett/J. Verheyden eds. *The Other Side: Apocryphal Perspectives on Ancient Christian 'Orthodoxies'* (NTOA/SUNT 117; Göttingen: Vandenhoeck & Ruprecht, 2017), 23-38.

Nordsieck, R., *Das Thomas-Evangelium. Einleitung. Die Frage nach dem historischen Jesus, Kommentierung aller 114 Logien* (4., durchgesehene und erweiterte Auflage; Neukirchen-Vluyn: Neukirchener Theologie, 2014).

Pagels, E., 'Exegesis of Genesis 1 in the Gospels of Thomas and John', in *JBL* 118 (1999), 477-496.

Pagels, E., *The Johannine Gospel in Gnostic Exegesis: Heracleon's commentary on John* (SBL.MS 17; Atlanta, Ga.: Scholars Press, 1989).

Pagels, E., *Das Geheimnis des fünften Evangeliums. Warum die Bibel nur die halbe Wahrheit sagt* (München: Beck, 2004).

Painter, J., *Just James. The brother of Jesus in history and tradition* (Personalities of the New Testament; Edinburgh: T & T Clark, 1999).

Patterson, S. J., *The Lost Way: How two forgotten Gospels are rewriting the story of Christian Origins* (New York: Harper One, 2014).

Patterson, S. J., 'The Gospel of Thomas and the Synoptic Tradition. A Forschungsbericht and Critique', in *Foundation and Facets Forum* 8 (1992), 45-97.

Patterson, S. J., 'Wisdom in Q and Thomas', in L. G. Perdue/B. B. Scott/W. J. Wiseman eds. *In search of wisdom, FS J. G. Gammie* (Louisville, Ky.: Westminster/John Knox Pr. 1993), 187-221.

Patterson, S. J., 'Understanding the gospel of Thomas today', in Idem/J. M. Robinson, James M, eds. *The fifth gospel. The gospel of Thomas comes of age* (Harrisburg, Penn.: Trinity Press Internat., 1998), 33-75.

Patterson, S. J./J. M. Robinson, eds. *The fifth gospel. The gospel of Thomas comes of age* (Harrisburg, Penn.: Trinity Press Internat., 1998).

Patterson, S. J., *The Gospel of Thomas and Jesus* (Foundations & facets. Reference series; Salem, Oregon: Polebridge Press, 1993).

Patterson, S. J., *The Gospel of Thomas and Christian Origins: Essays on the fifth Gospel* (NHMS 84; Leiden: Brill, 2013).

Patterson, S. J., 'Now playing: The gospel of Thomas', in *Bible review* 16 (2000), 38-41, 51-52.

Patterson, S. J., 'The Gospel of Thomas and the Historical Jesus', in A. Gregory/C. Tuckett, eds. *The Oxford Handbook of Early Christian Apocrypha* (Oxford: Oxford University Press 2015), 233-249.

Patterson, S. J., 'Jesus meets Plato: The Theology of the Gospel of Thomas and Middle Platonism', in: J. Frey/E. E. Popkes/J. Schröter (Hg.), *Das Thomasevangelium: Entstehung – Rezeption – Theologie* (BZNW 157; Berlin/New York: de Gruyter 2008), 181-205.

Pearson, B. A., 'Art. Nag Hammadi', in *AncB.D* IV (1992), 982-993.

Perrin, N., *Thomas und Tatian: the relationship between the Gospel of Thomas and the Diatessaron* (SBL.AB 5; Atlanta, Ga.: Scholars Press, 2002).

Perrin, N., 'NHC II,2 and the Oxyrhynchus Fragments (P.Oxy 1, 654, 655): overlooked evidence for a Syriac Gospel of Thomas', in *VigChr* 58 (2004), 138-151.

Perrin, N., 'The Aramaic Origins of the Gospel of Thomas – Revisited', in J. Frey/E. E. Popkes/J. Schröter, eds. *Das Thomasevangelium: Entstehung – Rezeption – Theologie* (BZNW 157; Berlin: Walter de Gruyter, 2008), 50-59.

Plisch, U.-K., *Das Thomasevangelium: Originaltext mit Kommentar* (Stuttgart: Deutsche Bibelgesellschaft, 2007).

Poirier, P.-H., '*Évangile* de Thomas, Actes de Thomas, Livre de Thomas. Une tradition et ses transformations', in *Apocrypha* 7 (1996), 9-26.

Poirier, P.-H., 'The writings ascribed to Thomas and the Thomas tradition', in J. D. Turner/A. McGuire, eds. *The Nag Hammadi li-*

brary after fifty years. Proceedings of the 1995 Society of Biblical Literature commemoration (NHS 44; Leiden/New York/Köln: Brill, 1997), 295-307.

Popkes, E. E., '"Ich bin das Licht" – Erwägungen zur Verhältnisbestimmung des Thomasevangeliums und der johanneischen Schriften anhand der Lichtmetaphorik', in J. Frey/U. Schnelle, eds. *Kontexte des Johannesevangeliums. Das vierte Evangelium in religions- und traditionsgeschichtlicher Perspektive* (WUNT 175; Tübingen: Mohr Siebeck, 2004), 641-674.

Popkes, E. E., *Das Menschenbild des Thomasevangeliums: Untersuchungen zu seiner religionshistorischen und chronologischen Verortung* (WUNT 206; Tübingen: Mohr Siebeck, 2007).

Popkes, E. E., *Erfahrungen göttlicher Liebe. Band 1: Nahtoderfahrungen als Zugänge zum Platonismus und zum frühen Christentum* (Göttingen: Vandenhoeck & Ruprecht, 2017).

Popkes, E. E., *Die Theologie der Liebe Gottes in den johanneischen Schriften: Studien zur Semantik der Liebe und zum Motivkreis des Dualismus* (WUNT II 197; Tübingen: Mohr Siebeck, 2005).

Popkes, E. E., 'Die Umdeutung des Todes Jesu im koptischen Thomasevangelium', in J. Schröter/J. Frey, eds. *Deutungen des Todes Jesu im Neuen Testament* (WUNT 181; Tübingen: Mohr Siebeck, 2005), 513-543.

Popkes, E. E., 'Von der Eschatologie zur Protologie: Die Transformation apokalyptischer Motive im Thomasevangelium', in M. Becker/M. Öhler, eds. *Apokalyptik als Herausforderung neutestamentlicher Theologie* (WUNT II 214; Tübingen: Mohr Siebeck, 2005), 213-235.

Popkes, E. E., 'About the differing approach to a theological heritage: Comments on the relationship between Qumran, the Gospel of John and the Gospel of Thomas', in J. Charlesworth u. a., eds. *The Bible and the Dead Sea Scrolls, Vol. III: Qumran and Christian Origins* (Waco, Tex.: Baylor Univ. Press, 2006), 271-309.

Popkes, E. E., 'Das Mysterion der Botschaft Jesu: Beobachtungen zur synoptischen Parabeltheorie und ihren Analogien im Johannesevangelium und Thomasevangelium', in R. Zimmermann, ed. *Hermeneutik der Gleichnisse Jesu. Methodische Neuansätze zum Verstehen urchristlicher Parabeltexte* (WUNT 231; Tübingen: Mohr Siebeck, 2008), 294-320.

Popkes, E. E., *Platonic Christianity: Historical and methodical foundations* (Platonic Christianty 1; Norderstedt: Book on Demand, 2020).

Popkes, E. E., 'The Image Character of human existence: GThom 83 and GThom 84 as core texts of the anthropology of the Gospel of Thomas', in J. Frey/E. E. Popkes/J. Schröter, eds. *Das Thomasevangelium: Entstehung – Rezeption – Theologie* (BZNW 157; Berlin/New York: Walter de Gruyter, 2008), 413-431.

Popkes, E. E., 'Das Thomasevangelium als crux interpretum: die methodischen Ursachen einer diffusen Diskussionslage', in J. Frey/J. Schröter, eds. *Jesus in apokryphen Evangelienüberlieferungen* (WUNT 254; Tübingen: Mohr Siebeck, 2010), 271-292.

Popkes, E. E., 'The Gospel of Thomas within Early Christian History: a Theological Appreciation and Discussion', in H. Assel/S. Beyerle/C. Böttrich, eds. *Beyond Biblical Theology* (WUNT 295; Tübingen: Mohr Siebeck, 2012), 609-625.

Popkes, E. E., 'Glaube und Erkenntnis: die Soteriologie des Johannesevangeliums und des Thomasevangeliums als Kontrast- und Konkurrenzkonzepte', in J. Frey/B. Schliesser/N. Ueberschaer, eds. *Glaube im frühen Christentum* (WUNT 373; Tübingen: Mohr Siebeck, 2017), 773-790.

Pratscher, W., *Der Herrenbruder Jakobus und die Jakobustradition* (FRLANT 139; Göttingen: Vandenhoeck & Ruprecht, 1987).

Riley, G. J., *Resurrection Reconsidered. Thomas and John in Controversy* (Minneapolis: Fortress, 1995).

Robinson, J. M., 'On Bridging the Gulf from Q to the Gospel of Thomas (or Vice Versa)', in C. W. Hedrick/R. Hodgson, eds. *Nag Hammadi, Gnosticism, & Early Christianity* (Peabody, Mass.: Hendrickson Publishers, 1986), 127-175.

Robinson, J. M./P. Hoffmann/J. S. Kloppenborg (ed.), *The Critical Edition of Q. Synopsis including the Gospel of Matthew and Luke, Mark and Thomas with English, German and French Translations of Q and Thomas* (Leuven/Minneapolis: Peeters, 2000).

Robinson, J. M., *The Discovering and Marketing of Coptic Manuscripts: The Nag Hammadi Codices and the Bodmer Papyri* (The roots of egyptian christianity = Studies in Antiquity and Christianity; Philadelphia: Fortress, 1986).

Robinson, J. M., 'Nag Hammadi: The first fifty years', in idem/S. J. Patterson, eds. *The fifth gospel. The gospel of Thomas comes of age* (Harrisburg, Pa.: Trinity Press International, 1998), 77-110.

Robinson, J. M., 'LOGOI SOPHON: zur Gattung der Spruchquelle Q', in H. Koester/J. M. Robinson, *Entwicklungslinien durch die Welt des frühen Christentums* (Tübingen: Mohr Siebeck, 1971), 67-106.

Röhser, G., *Prädestination und Verstockung: Untersuchungen zur frühjüdischen, paulinischen und johanneischen Theologie* (TANZ 14; Tübingen/Basel 1994).

Schenke, H.-M., 'On the compositional history of the Gospel of Thomas', in *FORUM* 10,1/2 (1994), 9-30.

Roig Lanzillotta, L., 'Gospel of Thomas Logion 7 Unravelled: an intertextual approach to a locus vexatus', in M. Baucks/W. Horowitz/A. Lange, eds. *Between Text and Text: The Hermeneutics of Intertextuality in Ancient Cultures and their Afterlife in Medieval and Modern Times* (JAJ.S 6; Göttingen: Vandenhoeck & Ruprecht, 2013), 116-132.

Schenke, H.-M., 'Das Buch des Thomas', in W. Schneemelcher, ed. *Neutestamentliche Apokryphen in deutscher Übersetzung*, 6. Aufl. (Tübingen: Mohr Siebeck, 1990), 192-204.

Schenke, H.-M., 'Das Buch des Thomas (NHC II,7)', in idem, *Nag Hammadi Deutsch (hrsg. durch die Berlin-Brandenburgische Akademie der Wissenschaften, eingeleitet und übersetzt von Mitgliedern des Berliner Arbeitskreises für Koptisch-Gnostische Schriften; hrsg. von H.-M. Schenke/H.-G. Bethge/U. U. Kaiser) Koptische-gnostische Schriften 2: NHC 1,1-5,1* (GCS N. F., Bd. 8; Berlin; New York: Walter de Gruyter 2001), 279-291.

Schenke, H.-M., *Das Thomas-Buch. Nag-Hammadi-Codex II/7* (TU 138, Berlin: Walter de Gruyter, 1989).

Schenke, H.-M., 'Platon, Politeia 588A-589B (NHC VI,5)', in H.-M. Schenke, *Nag Hammadi Deutsch (hrsg. durch die Berlin-Brandenburgische Akademie der Wissenschaften, eingeleitet und übersetzt von Mitgliedern des Berliner Arbeitskreises für Koptisch-Gnostische Schriften; hrsg. von H.-M. Schenke/H.-G. Bethge/U. U. Kaiser), Koptische-gnostische Schriften 3: NHC V,1-XIII,1* (GCS N. F. 12; Berlin/New York: Walter de Gruyter, 2003), 495-497.

Schenke, H.-M., 'Art. Nag Hammadi', in *TRE* 28 (1994), 731-736.

Schnelle, U., *Paulus. Leben und Denken* (de Gruyter Lehrbuch; Berlin: Walter de Gruyter, 2003).

Schnelle, U., *Einleitung in das Neue Testament* (UTB 1830; Göttingen: Vandenhoeck & Ruprecht, 2017[9]).

Schröter, J., *Erinnerung an Jesu Worte. Studien zur Rezeption der Logienüberlieferung in Markus, Q und Thomas* (WMANT 76; Neukirchen-Vluyn: Neukirchener Verlag, 1997).

Schröter, J., 'Die Herausforderung einer theologischen Interpretation des Thomasevangelium', in J. Frey/E. E. Popkes/J. Schröter, eds. *Das Thomasevangelium: Entstehung – Rezeption – Theologie* (BZNW 157; Berlin: Walter de Gruyter, 2008), 435-459.

Schröter, J./C. Jacobi, eds. *Jesus-Handbuch* (Handbücher Theologie; Tübingen: Mohr Siebeck, 2017).

Schur, B. T., *'Von hier nach dort': Der Philosophiebegriff bei Platon* (Göttingen: Vandenhoeck & Ruprecht, 2013).

Sellew, P., 'The Gospel of Thomas: Prospects for future research', in J. D. Turner/A. McGuire, eds. *The Nag Hammadi library after fifty years. Proceedings of the 1995 Society of Biblical Literature commemoration* (NHS 44; Leiden/New York/Köln: Brill, 1997), 327-346.

Sellew, P., 'Death, the body, and the world in the Gospel of Thomas', in *StPatr* 30 (1997), 530-534.

Sellew, P., 'Thomas Christianity: Scholars in quest of a community', in J. N. Bremmer, eds. *The apocryphal Acts of Thomas* (Studies on early christian apocrypha 6, Leuven: Peeters 2001), 11-35.

Szlezák, T. A., 'Der Begriff ‚Seele' als Mitte der Philosophie Platons', in K. Crone/R. Schnepf/J. Stolzenberg, eds. Über *die Seele* (Suhrkamp Taschenbuch 1916; Berlin: Suhrkamp, 2010), 13-34.

Theißen, G., *A theory of primitive Christian religion* (London: SCM Press: 2003).

Theißen, G./A. Merz, *Der historische Jesus: ein Lehrbuch* (Göttingen: Vandenhoeck & Ruprecht, 2013⁴).

Thomaskutty, J., *Saint Thomas the Apostle: New Testament, Apocrypha, and historical traditions* (Jewish and Christian Textes 25; London/New York/New Delhi/Sydney: Bloomsbury, 2018).

Thomassen, E., *The Spiritual Seed: the Church of the ‚Valentinians'* (Leiden/Boston: Brill, 2008²).

Thyen, H., *Das Johannesevangelium* (HNT 6; Tübingen: Mohr Siebeck, 2015²).

Tornau, C., 'Neuplatonische Kritik an den Gnostikern und das theologische Profil des Thomasevangeliums', in J. Frey/E. E. Popkes/J. Schröter, eds. *Das Thomasevangelium: Entstehung – Rezeption – Theologie* (BZNW 157; Berlin: Walter de Gruyter, 2008), 326-359.

Trillhaas, W., *Dogmatik* (4. verb. Auflage; Berlin: Walter de Gruyter, 1980, Reprint 2017).

Tubach, J., 'Historische Elemente in den Thomasakten', in idem/G. V. Vashalomidze, eds. *Studien zu den Thomas-Christen in Indien* (Hallesche Beiträge zur Orientwissenschaft 33 (Berlin: LIT, 2006), 49-116.

Tuckett, C., 'What's in a Name? How apocryphal are the apocryphal gospels', in T. Nicklas/C. R. Moss/C. Tuckett/J. Verheyden, eds. *The Other Side: Apocryphal Perspectives on Ancient Christian „Orthodoxies"* (NTOA/SUNT 117; Göttingen: Vandenhoeck & Ruprecht, 2017), 149-164.

Tuckett, C., 'Das Thomasevangelium und die synoptischen Evangelien', in *BThZ 12* (1995), 186-200.

Tuckett, C., 'The Gospel of Thomas: Evidence for Jesus?' in *NedThT* 52 (1998), 17-32.

Tuckett, C., 'Thomas and the Synoptics', in *NT* 30 (1998), 132-157.

Turner, J. D., *Sethian Gnosticism and the Platonic Tradition* (BCNH.É 6; Québec/Louvain-Paris: Presses de l'Univ. Laval, 2001).

Turner, J. D., 'Art. Valentinianism', in *AncB.D 6* (1992), 781-783.

Uro, R., 'Is Thomas an Encratite gospel?', in R. Uro, eds. *Thomas at the crossroads. Essays on the Gospel of Thomas* (Studies of the New Testament and its world; Edinburgh: Clark, 1998), 140-162.

Uro, R., *Thomas. Seeking the historical context of the Gospel of Thomas* (London: Clark, 2003).

Uro, R., 'Thomas at the crossroads. New perspectives on a debated gospel', in R. Uro, ed. *Thomas at the crossroads. Essays on the Gospel of Thomas* (Studies of the New Testament and its world; Edinburgh: Clark 1998), 1-7.

Valantasis, R., *The Gospel of Thomas* (New Testament Readings; London/New York: Routledge, 1997).

Williams, M. A., *Rethinking ‚Gnosticism'. An argument for dismantling a dubious category* (Princeton: Princeton Univ. Press, 1996).

Wisse, F., 'Gnosticism and Early Monasticism in Egypt', in B. Aland, eds. *Gnosis* (FS H. Jonas; Göttingen: Vandenhoeck & Ruprecht, 1978), 431-440.

Witischeck, S., *Thomas und Johannes – Johannes und Thomas. Das Verhältnisses der Logien des Thomasevangeliums zum Johannesevangelium* (HBS 79; Freiburg/Basel/Wien: Herder, 2015).

Wright, N. T., *The Resurrection of the Son of God* (London: SPCK, 2012).

Zander, H., *Geschichte der Seelenwanderung in Europa: alternative religiöse Traditionen von der Antike bis heute* (Darmstadt: Wissenschaftliche Buchgesellschaft, 1999).

Zeindler, W., *Erwählung: Gottes Weg in der Welt* (Zürich: TVZ, 2009).

Zimmermann, R., *Geschlechtermetaphorik und Gottesverhältnis: Traditionsgeschichte und Theologie eines Bildfelds in Urchristentum und antiker Umwelt* (WUNT II/122; Tübingen: Mohr Siebeck, 2001).

Zöckler, T., *Jesu Lehren im Thomasevangelium* (NHMS XLVII; Leiden/Boston/Köln: Brill, 1999).

Zumstein, J., *Das Johannesevangelium* (KEK 2; Göttingen: Vandenhoeck & Ruprecht, 2016).